THE ABANDONED GENERATION

The Abandoned Generation

RETHINKING HIGHER EDUCATION

William H. Willimon
and
Thomas H. Naylor

WILLIAM B. EERDMANS PUBLISHING COMPANY
GRAND RAPIDS, MICHIGAN

00 99 98 97 96 95   7 6 5 4 3 2 1

Library of Congress Cataloging-in-Publication Data

Willimon, William H.
The abandoned generation: rethinking higher education /
William H. Willimon and Thomas H. Naylor.
p.   cm.
Includes bibliographical references.
ISBN 0-8028-4119-8 (alk. paper)
1. Education, Higher — United States. 2. Universities and colleges —
United States — Sociological aspects. 3. College students — United States —
Conduct of life. 4. College students — United States — Attitudes.
I. Naylor, Thomas H., 1936–   . II. Title.
LA227.4.W56   1995
378.973 — dc20   95-20783
                                                 CIP

To

H. Keith H. Brodie

Contents

CONTENTS

Foreword

The station wagons arrived at noon, a long shining line that coursed through the west campus. In single file they eased around the orange I-beam sculpture and moved toward the dormitories. The roofs of the station wagons were loaded down with carefully secured suitcases full of light and heavy clothing; with boxes, blankets, boots and shoes, stationery and books, sheets, pillows, quilts; with rolled-up rugs and sleeping bags; with bicycles, skis, rucksacks, English and Western saddles, inflated rafts. As cars slowed to a crawl and stopped, students sprang out and raced to the rear doors to begin removing the objects inside; the stereo sets, radios, personal computers; small refrigerators and table ranges; the cartons of phonograph records and cassettes; the hairdryers and styling irons; the tennis rackets, soccer balls, hockey and lacrosse sticks, bows and arrows; the controlled substances, the birth control pills and devices; the junk food still in shopping bags — onion and garlic chips, nacho thins, peanut creme patties, Waffelos and Kabooms, fruit chews and toffee popcorn; the Dum Dum pops, and Mystic mints.

I've witnessed this spectacle every September for twenty-one years. It is a brilliant event, invariably.[1]

---

1. Don DeLillo, *White Noise* (New York: Penguin Books, 1984), p. 3.

Because we have given most of our adult lives to careers as university professors — participants in the September spectacle of students arriving on campus, casting their lot with us for the next four years — one might think this would be an easy book for us to write. Because we have had firsthand acquaintance with dozens of institutions of higher education, having served with a number of faculties, both of us representing the sweep of the modern university's concern — one of us in the humanities, the other in the social sciences — one might think it would be a relatively easy task for us to say something to the academic world in which we live. It was not.

Making general statements about something so rich and diverse as American higher education is difficult. While we have spent time on dozens of college and university campuses over the years, there are over 3,400 institutions of higher education in this country. It is tough to generalize. Saying potentially abrasive or unpopular things to our colleagues in the university and college is difficult, yes. But as professors, it has not been uncommon for us to be regarded, by our students and our colleagues, as both abrasive and unpopular. No, our real challenge has been to speak of an academic world in which we do not yet live, a world that we catch only in glimpses on our respective campuses, a world waiting to be born, if we have the courage to give it birth.

Trained in our respective disciplines to find the facts, to uncover reality and name it, to state what is as opposed to what is not, we now want to venture forth from the present situation on today's campus and talk not just about what is but also about what ought to be. We take some pride that our respective institutions, Middlebury and Duke, have taken specific, positive, innovative steps to move out of denial and to experiment with new forms of undergraduate education. Unlike all too many institutions of American higher education, our schools have taken a tough, honest look at themselves and have launched bold initiatives to address the situation. We offer this book as one aspect of our institutions' leadership in transforming American higher education.

We would not have written this book if not for our students, those whom we encountered in our classes, particularly in our team-taught course, "The Search for Meaning." In that course, we not only became friends with one another — an unlikely pair, a theologian and an economist — but we became friends with our students. In the time of that venture together, in listening to our students, in arguing with them about things that matter, in watching their adult lives unfold, in hearing their accounts of their college years, we became convinced that American higher education faces a crisis, that we are not meeting the educational needs of our students as we ought, and that, as faculty, we can do better.

So to our students, we offer this book. We would not be here without you; here advocating major reformation of higher education; here, late in our academic careers, speaking up for a bold change in direction for our colleges and universities. Because of our enjoyment of our students, we disassociate ourselves from the popular right-wing attacks upon today's colleges that have been written by people like Dinesh D'Souza and others.[2] These calls for a return to the allegedly "good old days" seem to us misguided. We want something more radical, more visionary.

We also offer this book in gratitude for the leadership of our friend and former president, H. Keith H. Brodie, M.D. Dr. Brodie not only encouraged us in our "Search for Meaning" class at Duke but also courageously asked one of us, Will, to do a report on student life at Duke. This began not only campus-wide discussions that yielded many good things at Duke but also caught us faculty up in a new concern for today's students. Keith Brodie is a master at encouraging faculty to give their best to their high calling as teachers.

---

2. Books that come to mind in this genre are Allan Bloom, *The Closing of the American Mind* (New York: Simon and Schuster, 1987); and Dinesh D'Souza, *Illiberal Education* (New York: Free Press, 1991). D'Souza's fulminations against radical indoctrination by "politically correct" professors overlook the fact that the modern college's groping attempts toward a recovery of the moral dimension of our education are urgently needed. As we shall argue later in this book (particularly in chapter 8), all education is, in a sense, indoctrination. Rather than ignore the question, What sort of human beings are we producing at our colleges and universities? we hope to foster a national discussion on our campuses about what sort of moral formation is occurring there.

He also made Duke a leader in honestly assessing undergraduate education in America. While he may disagree with much in this book, Dr. Brodie's leadership has been our inspiration.[3]

We admit that our experience of higher education, though comparatively extensive, is limited to places like Duke and Middlebury, though Tom has taught recently at the University of Vermont. Those who teach and learn at this nation's public universities, community colleges, and elsewhere will have to judge for themselves the relevance of our recommendations. Before they too quickly dismiss our ideas, we urge them to consider that, while we have not been on the faculties of these alternative institutions, we have had enough experience on your campuses to suggest to us that we share many of the same challenges.

To our students — we must not abandon you, for not only are you the face of tomorrow, you are also the font from which true renewal of higher education must flow. In conversation with you, in encountering you in all of your strange and wonderful talent and potential, we both have rediscovered the sacredness of our own vocation to teach.

To our students —

William H. Willimon
Thomas H. Naylor
1995

3. The rather phenomenal response to Will's article "Reaching and Teaching the Abandoned Generation," *The Christian Century,* 20 Oct. 1993, pp. 1016-17, provided the impetus for this book. The article reported on the results of the study Dr. Brodie initiated at Duke.

THE SYMPTOMS

I Can't Believe How Drunk
I Was Last Night

Sambo, it's a good faculty they've got at this college. A couple of them even taught me when I was there. The thing for you to do is work hard. . . . Now, there's one thing I want to caution you about. A lot of times they have pretty wild parties at college. Young boys can get wound up like clock springs; sometimes they just plain bust loose. That's understandable. But watch the liquor. There's some bad stuff being made around the country, and a man really needs to have a bootlegger he can trust. Some of that stuff will kill you and some of it will drive you wild. You've got bottled-in-bond available now, and it's a good idea to stick to that even if it does cost more.[1]

It is 2:00 A.M. I am standing next to a campus public safety officer on the quad amid a crowd of exuberant students who are watching embers die in a bonfire. The fire, fueled by a couple of benches dragged from various locations on campus, has been extinguished by public safety officers. During the waning hours of this night, I

1. Ferrol Sams, *The Whisper of the River* (New York: Penguin Books, 1986), pp. 18-19.

have talked with a number of students, many of whom were inebriated. I accompanied an officer as he broke up two fraternity parties
for violating noise restrictions. We escorted four football players out
of a party where they were not wanted. We interviewed a student
who had been chased back to his room by lead-pipe-swinging community hooligans. Then we answered an anonymous complaint that
someone was "beating up his girlfriend in the room next door." By
the time we arrived, no one wanted to talk. We left.

The weather has become cold as Saturday becomes Sunday. A
group of students bids me farewell — "See ya, Reverend. Hope you
see some more action tomorrow night."

Why am I standing here, with people like this, on a night like
this? A short time before I had been summoned to the office of the
president, who told me he was increasingly concerned about student
life at our school — about alcohol abuse, residential life, students'
personal safety, social activities, fraternities, and sports, particularly
as these aspects of student life helped or hindered the school's
academic mission. Perceiving a gap between students' academic pur-
suits and their life after dark and on weekends, the president and
the provost asked me to listen to students, to gather information on
the relation between social and academic activities, and to report my
findings.

These findings, along with those of my collaborator Thomas
Naylor, provide the experiential basis for this book. Together we
created and taught "The Search for Meaning" seminar at Duke in
1991. We have offered the seminar every year since 1991, a seminar
that has provided us the opportunity for much in-depth interaction
with undergraduates. Naylor now lives in Vermont, where he teaches
at Middlebury College and the University of Vermont.

As providence would have it, the day after this project began,
Duke alumnus and professor of English Reynolds Price, in a
Founders' Day speech in Duke Chapel, delivered a broadside in
which he challenged his audience to "stand at a bus stop at noon
rush hour; roam the reading rooms of the libraries in the midst of
the term and panic of exams. Last, eat lunch in a dining hall and
note the subjects of conversation." Listeners would hear, said Price,

one sentence more than any other — "I can't believe how drunk I was last night."

Alcohol-related problems are in no way unique to our campus. On many campuses, free beer-keg parties provide the energy and focus for campus social life. Kegs have resulted in a steady stream of alcohol-related emergency-room visits by students, reports of alcohol counseling, and extensive damage to residence halls. Nation-wide, alcohol is a factor in the majority of the rapes among college-age students. We believe that student alcohol abuse is symptomatic of deeper malaise. Alcohol abuse is an illusory attempt to deal with their separation and meaninglessness.

> Sing to the colors that float in the light,
>   Hurrah for the yellow and blue!
> Yellow the stars as they ride through the night,
> And reel in a rollicking crew. . . .
> > University of Michigan alma mater

It is safe to assume that the "rollicking crew" were drunk.

To a startled alumni group an enthusiastic Duke senior proclaimed, "Duke University is a world-class university, far superior to Princeton. It is one of the few major universities where it is possible to get drunk four nights a week for four years and still maintain a B-average."

To support this claim, the student cited the recent visit of several friends from Princeton who confirmed that Duke is indeed a premier party school. Is this what the author of a cover-page article in the *New York Times Magazine* had in mind when he described Duke as a "hot college"?

However, an article in the *Princeton Alumni Weekly* by D. W. Miller, entitled "Saying When: Princeton Faces Its Drinking Problem,"[2] casts doubt on Duke's alleged competitive advantage. Sur-

2. "Saying When: Princeton Faces Its Drinking Problem," *Princeton Alumni Weekly*, November 25, 1992.

veys show that 80 percent of Princeton students drink, and 35 percent are "binge drinkers" — they regularly consume five or more drinks at one sitting. When an intoxicated freshman fell from the roof of Campbell Hall in 1985, his death produced little action. This event was followed by two other episodes: a weekend binge in 1988 in which 40 students were treated for alcohol abuse by the Princeton Student Clinic; and the electrocution of a Princeton sophomore in 1990 while climbing drunk atop the Dinky Shuttle late at night, leading to the amputation of three of his limbs and prompting Princeton president Harold Shapiro to declare alcohol abuse "the single greatest threat to the university's fulfillment of its mission."

The social scene at Duke or Princeton differs little from that at hundreds of other American colleges and universities. The widely publicized University of Virginia fraternity-house drug raids followed by reports of female striptease artists performing oral sex to entertain freshman rushees represent more of the same. College students suffer from a more fundamental malaise than alcohol and drug abuse. Their lives are meaningless.

The University of Vermont (UVM) now holds the dubious honor of leading all other colleges and universities in alcohol and drug abuse, a U.S. Department of Education survey has determined.[3] According to the study, 57.7 percent of UVM students under the age of twenty-one admitted to binge drinking at least once during the two-week period prior to the survey, compared to the national average of 47.5 percent. Furthermore, 40.6 percent binged at least twice during the same two-week period compared to 33 percent for the country as a whole. Among twenty-one-year-olds and older, 49 percent binged during the survey period compared to 35 percent for the nation.

On average, UVM students consume 6.5 drinks a week compared to 5.3 drinks nationally for students attending four-year colleges. Somewhat surprisingly, the survey found that students at smaller colleges such as Middlebury, with fewer than 2,500 students,

3. As reported in the University of Vermont *Cynic*.

drink an average of 6.9 drinks a week while students at larger institutions, with more than 20,000 students, drink 4.3 drinks per week on average. The big, impersonal university is not sufficient explanation for abuse. The small college, with its tighter sense of community and perhaps more rigidly enforced social norms, is a good breeding ground for abuse of alcohol.

One particularly troubling disclosure in the UVM study was the fact that 37.1 percent of UVM students drove while intoxicated or under the influence once a year, and 9.4 percent admitted to doing so six to nine times a year. Eighteen percent of UVM students acknowledged taking sexual advantage of somebody else as a result of drinking. Not surprisingly, UVM is ranked the third-best party school in the nation by *Playboy* and *Inside Edge,* a student-run magazine based in Boston. Alcohol was a contributing factor in the deaths of four UVM students in five years.

A 1993 University of Michigan study on alcohol abuse notes that "Immoderate drinking has long been a distinguishing element of college and university culture."[4] Drunkenness was prominent in European universities by the eighteenth century. American colleges and universities followed their old world ancestors in this as in other traditions. The Michigan study cites Romberg's well-known operetta, *The Student Prince,* which gave musical expression to the exalted place of alcohol in academic culture. Though set in Heidelberg, it was written by an American and had its greatest success on this side of the Atlantic. Yale's well-known "Whiffenpoof Song" celebrates the joys of collegiate drinking.

In 1994, a commission convened by the Center on Addiction and Substance Abuse at Columbia University, with former Department of Health, Education, and Welfare secretary Joseph A. Califano, Jr., as chair, issued a rather alarmist report, "Rethinking Rites of Passage: Substance Abuse on America's Campuses."[5] It noted that now one in three college students drinks primarily to get drunk.

---

4. Cited in Henry Wechsler et al., "Too Many Colleges Are Still in Denial about Alcohol Abuse," *The Chronicle of Higher Education,* April 14, 1995, p. B1.
5. As reported in *The New York Times,* June 11, 1994, p. 21.

The number of women who reported drinking to get drunk more than tripled between 1977 and 1993, a rate now equal to that of men.

Alcohol abuse turns out to be a much more complex subject than it first appeared to us. It cannot be attributed simply to adolescent exuberance or rowdiness or, in the case of male college students, to the aphorism "boys will be boys." It is not enough to say, "This is nothing new; students have always behaved this way."

Today alcohol appears to fulfill certain "social functions" beyond the simple narcotic effect of taking away adolescent social anxiety. There is, for example, a significant commercial component to youths' consumption of alcohol. According to the U.S. surgeon general, our country's college students drink nearly four billion cans of beer and enough wine and liquor to bring their annual consumption of alcoholic beverages up to thirty-four gallons a person. The Califano report noted that college students spend a total of $5.5 billion a year on alcohol, more than on all other beverages and their books combined. The average student spends $446 on alcohol per year, far exceeding the per capita expenditure for the college library. Not surprisingly, the beer industry targets young adults as its best hope for increasing sales. Thus National Collegiate Athletic Association (NCAA) basketball is brought to us by Anheuser Busch. On campus we speak of "TV revenues" from intercollegiate athletics. We mean "beer revenue." One rarely sees anyone our age in a beer commercial. Beer consumption has been declining among adult Americans each year for the past decade except for one group of adults — college-age students, many of whom are under the legal drinking age. It is sad that our students, who ought to be among the nation's most thoughtful, are so easily manipulated by sophisticated Madison Avenue gurus.

Your Good Friends at Budweiser

North Carolina basketball coach Dean Smith scolded the presidents of ACC schools . . . saying only one responded to his call to ban beer advertisements from televised college games.

"It's a shame that the worst problem they have on the campuses now is alcohol consumption," Smith said. "I'm not telling anyone to not have a beer, but through the years I've asked the presidents of the ACC to do away with the silly ads that say, 'And now, a word from our good friends at Budweiser.' . . ."[6]

Alcohol also serves to demarcate certain social groups. Students living in fraternities or sororities have an average of fifteen drinks per week, compared to only five drinks per week by other students. Affluence and the amount of discretionary time are contributing factors in alcohol consumption. The Califano report noted that white males drink far more than any other campus group, averaging more than nine drinks per week — over twice the rate of their female counterparts and nearly three times more than African-American male students. When African-American students on our campus were asked why they chose to live together in a residential area known as Central Campus, preference for an Afrocentric environment was not their answer. Instead, they cited alcohol abuse in the dorms. The vomit on the floor during the entire weekend and the condition of the restrooms after a night of partying send a clear signal: "This is an exclusive, white drinking club. You are not wanted here."

6. "Smith Calls for End to Beer Ads," *Durham Herald-Sun,* September 30, 1994.

9

White male students drink nine times more per week than African-American female students. Yet on campuses where African-Americans are in a majority, administrators report binge-drinking patterns similar to that on predominantly white campuses. An African-American sophomore demonstrated the possible racial and economic component of alcohol abuse or avoidance:

I Don't Drink

Why do I not drink? I'll put it to you this way. I am the first person in my family to come to a university. As an African-American male, my chances of death are higher now than they will be again until I'm 80, if I live until I'm 80. I've got stuff to do. That's why I don't go to kegs.

Duke University junior

Since male students often use alcohol to raise their sexual courage to approach women, it was not surprising to find that many women students feel threatened by the alcoholic environment on campus. One woman challenged me "to come over and spend a night in our dorm and listen to the sort of things I have to listen to every weekend night. It's scary." I did. It was.

The Califano report notes that 95 percent of all violent crime on campus is alcohol-related. Ninety percent of all reported campus rapes occur when alcohol is being used by either the assailant or the victim. Sixty percent of college women who have acquired sexually transmitted diseases, including AIDS and genital herpes, were under the influence of alcohol at the time they had intercourse. It may be more academically acceptable to speak of rape as a women's issue, a gender power issue, but that may be deflecting us from campus violence as an alcohol issue.

A 1994 Harvard School of Public Health study, as reported in the *Journal of the American Medical Association,* highlighted the effects of alcohol abusers upon their fellow students.[7] At schools where drinking was popular, more than two-thirds of the students had their sleep or study interrupted by drunken peers. More than a fourth of the students surveyed on the study's 140 campuses reported an unwanted sexual advance by an inebriated student. The disregard drunken students have for their fellow students, coupled with the unwillingness of sober students to confront the behavior of their drunken classmates, highlights the breakdown of community on the campus.

The Most Serious Student Problem

[A]lcohol is the most serious problem facing the students at Washington and Lee. . . . As drinking goes up, grades go down.[8]

We do not say college drinking is worse today than yesterday, although the statistics do suggest that a major new factor in student drunkenness is the growing percentage of women who binge-drink. Perhaps the main difference today is that the social *consequences* of alcohol abuse are no longer considered socially unacceptable. We may have a better understanding of the long-term effects of alcohol. Many of the devastating consequences of student alcohol abuse do not show up until later in adulthood. More than 300,000 of today's 12 million undergraduates will ultimately die from alcohol-related causes — more than the number who will earn MAs and PhDs combined.

7. As reported in the *Burlington Free Press,* November 11, 1994. See also Wechsler et al., pp. B1-B2.
8. David Howison, dean of students, Washington and Lee, in "Alcohol Survey Released, Shows Major Abuses," *Ring-tum Phi,* October 14, 1994, p. 1.

Fortunately some colleges are experimenting with "substance-free" dormitories for the students who do not wish to live amid the consequences of binge drinking. Too many schools — in response to market pressures — are so preoccupied with enrollment levels, competitive advantage, careerism, cost control, internationalism, and multicultural pluralism that they have little understanding of the root causes of students' substance abuse. Inadequate parenting, separation, alienation, economic uncertainty, and meaninglessness all contribute to drunken fraternity-house bashes, date rape, vandalism, and acts of violence. One Valentine's Day a couple of years ago, the two lead stories of the daily student newspaper were the indictment of one of our students for date rape and a student barroom knifing brawl. And these are the leaders of tomorrow?

There are some encouraging signs that alcohol abuse may have begun to decline on campus. One in four students reported abstaining from alcohol in 1971. Today nearly half of all college students say they abstain, according to a nationwide study by the University of California at Los Angeles.[9] Alas, binge drinking appears to be on the rise. More colleges must join schools like Duke, Princeton, Washington and Lee, and Michigan in their bold attempts to address this pressing problem.

Economics 101

My old man busted his butt for the company, then, when he turns fifty, the company calls him in and says, "We don't need you anymore." They call it "downsizing." I call it getting screwed by the company. I don't want to end my life like my old man.

Birmingham-Southern College senior

---

9. "Drinking Losing Popularity with College Students," *Durham Herald-Sun*, February 5, 1995, p. A13.

In the present economic context, many students feel they have little incentive to delay gratification because they place so little faith in an uncertain future that has no meaning for them. Instead, they pursue the more immediate desire "to have it all and to have it now" — a dream that turns out to be a lie, a materialistic cover for a lack of meaning.

While subscribing to an ideology that raises individualism as the supreme human value, most college students behave as docile conformists. Some have tried — often in vain — to find meaning through the approval of parents, excessive television viewing, rock music, spectator sports, physical fitness, sexual promiscuity, and racism. Ironically, lacking a sense of direction, a firm conviction about what their lives ought to mean, they become the compliant victims of external pressures. Their parents, their passions, and the corporation pull their strings.

The college campus mirrors the conclusions of a study by the American Medical Association and the National Association of State Boards of Education. "Never before has one generation of American teen-agers been less healthy, less cared-for or less prepared for life than their parents were at the same age."[10]

The rate of violent crimes by youth in the United States rose by 25 percent during the 1980s. The teenage suicide rate has tripled over the past three decades. Suicide is the second-leading cause of death of fifteen- to nineteen-year-olds. A Gallup Poll found that 15 percent of American teenagers have seriously considered suicide and that 6 percent have actually tried it. Over 70 percent of teenage suicides involve the frequent use of alcohol or drugs.

---

10. Quoted in T. H. Naylor, W. H. Willimon, and M. R. Naylor, *The Search for Meaning* (Nashville: Abingdon, 1994), p. 12.

On the Other Side of the Atlantic

There were a number of subject drinks parties [parties for physics majors or language majors, etc.] in rooms in the college yesterday evening. The excessively intense alcohol consumption to which all students, but especially freshers, are subjected on these occasions is a serious threat to health. . . . This threat to health, along with the noise disturbance, and the very considerable vomit pollution, makes such events completely unacceptable.

Note from the senior dean, posted on the bulletin board,
Keble College, Oxford, January 1995

We believe that campus life is a metaphor for our national malaise — meaninglessness. Too much leisure time has given college students more freedom than they can consume. Paraphrasing what Eric Fromm once said about our society as a whole, college students are notoriously unhappy people — lonely, anxious, depressed, destructive, dependent — who are glad when they have killed the time they were trying so hard to save.

The point of this tale is not to condemn alcohol on college campuses. Both of us participated actively in the social life of our respective college fraternities. Indeed, as part of the initiation ceremony into an engineering fraternity at Columbia University in the 1950s, Tom paraded around Times Square somewhat inebriated for several hours with a funeral wreath around his neck. Now in middle age, we have learned that alcohol is far from a neutral or normal aspect of adolescent life.

Campus alcohol abuse is indicative of a plethora of social, psychological, and economic problems confronting today's college students. Broken homes, teachers who don't teach, the failure to integrate the residential and academic components of college life, the professionalization of college athletics, grade inflation, cur-

14

riculum sprawl, and the absence of community on campus are all important pieces of the puzzle. But above all is the abandonment by higher education of the moral, character-related aspects of education, the widespread but, we believe, erroneous assumption on the part of administrators that it is possible to have a college or a university without having an opinion of what sort of people ought to be produced by that institution.

Reality Test

I just got the shit scared out of me. I went into the CD Store to buy a CD I've been wanting. The guy who waited on me was wearing a Duke ring! I told him I was at Duke now and he says, "Lots of luck. I hope you'll have better luck than I did peddling my degree."

Duke University sophomore

The three most visible symptoms of the crisis in higher education are (1) substance abuse, (2) indolence, and (3) excessive careerism. Underlying these symptoms are three fundamental problems: (1) meaninglessness; (2) fragmentation of a student's life into un-related, incoherent components; and (3) the absence of community.

The Culture of Neglect

Among my experiences as a college president is the all-too-frequent phone call in the night that begins: "One of your students is in the emergency room with alcohol poisoning." The whole country got a similar wake-up call in June when it was reported that alcohol abuse on college campuses is on the rise, especially for women, and that college students drink far more than nonstudents. One statistic showed that college students spend more money on alcohol while in college than on books.

Alcohol abuse, although tragic, is but one symptom of a larger campus crisis. A generation has come to college quite fragile, not very secure about who it is, fearful of its lack of identity, and without confidence in its future. Many students are ashamed of themselves and afraid of relationships.

Students use alcohol as an escape. It's used as an excuse for bad behavior: the insanity defense writ large on campus. This diminished sense of self has caused a growth in racism, sexism, assault, date rape, attempted suicide, eating disorders, theft, property damage and cheating on most campuses.

This is not the stuff of most presidents' public conversations. Nor can it be explained away as an "underclass" problem; it is found on our most privileged campuses. It is happening because the generation now entering college has experienced few authentic connections with adults in its lifetime. I call this the "Culture of Neglect," and we — parents, teachers, professors, and administrators — are the primary architects.

It begins at home, where social and economic factors — such as declining wages and stagnating incomes requiring longer work hours — result in less family time. Young people have been allowed to or must take part-time jobs rather than spending time in school, on homework or with their families. More children and adolescents are being reared in a vacuum, with television as their only supervisor, and there is little expectation that they learn personal responsibility. Immersed in themselves, they're left to their peers.

We have failed to teach an ethic of concern and to model a culture of responsibility. We have created a culture characterized by dysfunctional families, mass schooling that demands only minimal effort and media idols subliminally teaching disrespect for authority and wisdom. It is as if there were a conspiracy of parents and educators to deliberately ruin our children. College students reared in the culture of neglect externalize any notion of obligation and responsibility. Listen to Leon Botstein, president of Bard College, in *Harper's* magazine: ". . . students through the 1960s accepted the idea that higher education was about trying on the clothes of adulthood, so they eagerly accepted responsibility for their actions. If . . . they got drunk, if they hurt someone, they sought to take responsibility. Today's students believe they are not responsible; quite the opposite . . . they feel they are *owed* something."

There is some parental involvement. I, and other college presidents, receive from "caring" parents angry letters, phone calls, and threats of legal action, all demanding acknowledgement of their children's victimization. I had one late-night call from a parent wanting to know "how can it be possible that my son received an F." Another parent complained that "with such high tuition it is the college's responsibility to provide a lawyer for students when they are arrested by city police after presenting false ID." On an admissions tour, a parent angrily left the campus upon learning that we did not provide cable-TV hookups in residence halls.

Colleges and universities must accept some responsibility for the culture of neglect, for we have succumbed to the lower standards of the larger culture. Faculty members and administrators have lowered their expectations, resulting in grade inflation. Intellectual demands placed on college students are less than they need or are capable of handling. Yet, despite low expectations and standards and plenty of free time, fewer than half of all students who enter college ever graduate, and those who do increasingly are seen by employers as having learned too little.

Campuses are in crisis and college presidents can provide

real leadership. Two years ago I warned our fraternity system that if it did not improve it would be abolished. A year later we closed one house for hazing violations and alcohol abuse. Parents and alumni of the banned brotherhood responded — lawyers were threatened; alumni said they would stop giving money; weeks were spent answering letters, phone calls, faxes, e-mail, all chanting a familiar refrain: "We did it when we were in school." "It's all part of bonding."

We persevered — a year later the alumni of that house have pledged to help us implement a yearly accreditation and evaluation system for fraternities. We are seeing a new brand of fraternity leadership, willing to meet our earlier challenge to excellence, even if some parents do not appreciate that we care enough to demand safe behavior. This is more than about fraternities — it's about higher standards. Administrators, faculty members, parents, alumni, and students have come together to take a step toward a more responsible campus culture.

A nation of individuals who cannot read or write well, with no sense of major human questions, who cannot think critically or show interest in learning and who are unable to act responsibly in a diverse democratic society will be ill equipped to compete in any new world order. A culture of neglect demands little. A culture of responsibility demands more from all of us but holds the promise of far greater rewards.[11]

To confront the problems of what we call the *abandoned generation* of college students, we shall consider four strategies: (1) restructuring the academy, (2) teachers who teach, (3) curriculum reform, and (4) the rediscovery of colleges and universities as learning communities.

11. Richard H. Hersh, president of Hobart College, "My Turn," *Newsweek*, November 15, 1994.

CHAPTER 2

We Work Hard, We Play Hard

It was shortly before midnight in early March; I had been entertaining the college intellectuals to mulled claret; the fire was roaring, the air of my room heavy with smoke and spice, and my mind weary with metaphysics. I threw open my windows and from the quad outside came the not uncommon sounds of bibulous laughter and unsteady steps. A voice said: "Hold up"; another, "Come on"; another, "Plenty of time . . . House . . . till Tom stops ringing"; and another, clearer than the rest, "D'you know I feel most unaccountably unwell. I must leave you a minute," and there appeared at my window the face I knew to be Sebastian's, but not, as I had formerly seen it, alive and alight with gaiety; he looked at me for a moment with unfocused eyes and then, leaning forward well into the room, he was sick.

It was not unusual for dinner parties to end in that way; there was in fact a recognized tariff for the scout on such occasions; we were all learning, by trial and error, to carry our wine.[1]

1. Evelyn Waugh, *Brideshead Revisited* (New York: Penguin Books, 1951), p. 31.

Nothing better characterizes the self-image of college students across the nation today than one of their favorite self-designations — "We work hard, we play hard." There is a widespread belief among students that not only do they play hard but they are hard-working as well.

Party On, Wayne

Does your son like to party? Then he'll love Washington and Lee. The school really attracts smart people, but they aren't nerds. Did you see the frat houses? Our motto is, "We work hard and we play hard."

Washington and Lee University sophomore

The graduating senior who proclaimed Duke a "world-class drinking school" in chapter 1 added, "But we work hard and we play hard." Do college students actually work very hard today? On a superficial level, how is it possible to work hard and maintain the lifestyle we described in the first chapter? On a more substantive level, we need to examine what has happened to college graduation requirements over the past twenty years.

We Play Hard

Look, this is nothing. We did the same thing last night and turned out for exams. We can handle it.

Cecily, a junior at the University of New Hampshire, downing her fourth beer while speaking to a reporter[2]

---

2. "Higher Education: Crocked on Campus," *Time*, December 19, 1994, p. 67.

When we were college students in the 1950s and 1960s, it was not uncommon to take six or seven courses each semester. Today the standard course load at many colleges and universities is only four courses per semester. Special permission is often required to take five. The gutting of college curricula was demanded and achieved by student leaders in the late sixties and early seventies in the name of increased freedom and flexibility. In theory, students were to take fewer courses, but the courses were to be more demanding, thus enabling them to concentrate their energies on a smaller number of subjects. In practice the requirements have actually become easier. At many institutions it became possible to graduate with little or no knowledge of mathematics, basic science, foreign language, history, philosophy, or religion. By the end of the 1980s, the significance of a college degree had greatly declined.

Another outgrowth of the "student movement" of the sixties (in which Will, as a student, was an active participant) contributing to reduced workloads and grade inflation was teacher-course evaluations. On the surface, teacher-course evaluations appear to be progressive, giving students the opportunity to provide professors with feedback on their teaching abilities without fear of reprisals. In reality, the course evaluations provide another incentive for professors to give high grades and make their courses easy.

In a nation shaped by television, sound bites, and video games with instant gratification, college students expect to be entertained by their professors. If a homework assignment requires more than fifteen minutes to complete, then there must be something wrong with the professor or the assignment. Even very bad teachers know that they can improve their ratings with their students by making their courses easy and giving good grades — particularly at the beginning of the course.

As professors, knowing that our salary may be influenced by our teacher-course evaluations may make us unwilling deliberately to risk poor student evaluations. We learn that it is best to avoid giving low grades on quizzes and papers before the teacher evaluation forms have been distributed at the end of the semester. An optimum strategy is gradually to improve the grades one gives a student during the course of the semester before he or she has a chance to evaluate. One should never overtly confront students about their class attendance, indolence, apathy, or impertinent behavior. The entire class may turn against the professor, leading to a precipitous drop in one's ratings as a teacher. But if one gives a student good grades early in the semester and then turns in a final grade of D or F, one is really asking for it. Since this course grade may determine whether or not a student gets into the graduate school of his or her choice, one can expect the wrath of the student and his or her parents. Parental pressure on faculty members for grades is not at all uncommon these days.

Quid Pro Quo

The students are telling us, "I pay so much to go to school here — you can't give me D's and F's!"[3]

Harvard professor William Cole has noted that the so-called gentleman's C has given way to the "gentleperson's B," a gracious stamp of approval for merely average work. At Harvard in 1992, 91 percent of undergraduate grades were B minus or higher. At Princeton, A's rose from 33 percent of all grades to 40 percent in four years. As *U.S. News and World Report* writer John Leo noted, "Give A's and B's for average effort and the whole system becomes a game of 'Let's Pretend.' Parents are pleased and don't keep the pressure on. Students tend to relax and expect high rewards for low output."[4]

3. Norman Wessells, University of Oregon provost, as quoted in "Give Me an A, or Give Me Death," *Newsweek,* June 13, 1994, p. 62.
4. *Harvard Alumni Magazine,* March 1993, p. 31.

Intellectual Climate

After arriving at the university, I quickly found myself caught up in the fraternity keg scene. I changed my wardrobe, my hairstyle, everything to suit the image I was trying to adopt. Then, when I went home over the holiday break, it hit me. The conversation around my family dinner table was far better than any conversation I had all semester at Duke. My family loves to talk and debate around the table. I said to myself, "This isn't you. What are you doing? You want something else." So I decided then and there that I would have to move off campus if I were to have the intellectual life I wanted. Duke students say, "We work hard and we play hard" — but do we say that we THINK hard? Are we really developing the critical thinking skills we need?

Duke University senior

Novelist Reynolds Price reports that in his all-elective classes, he now routinely encounters "the stunned or blank faces of students who exhibit a minimum of preparation or willingness for what I think of as the high delight and life-enduring pleasure of serious conversation in the classroom and elsewhere."

First-year students in Tom's seminar on "The New Economics of the Former Soviet Union and Eastern Europe" come to class well prepared and eager to participate in class discussion. It is a delight to teach such a seminar. But a similar course covering essentially the same material offered to *seniors* who have not taken the former course invokes a quite different response. The seniors often miss class, and when they are there, they are lethargic and contribute little to discussion. What do we do to them in four years to snuff out their intellectual flame?

The Almighty GPA

From what I hear, corporate recruiters only ask you one question, "What was your overall GPA?" They're desperate for some way to weed out job applicants, I guess. So a person is a fool to take the hard courses, to risk screwing up your GPA because you took some course for its "intellectual content" or other such crap.

Haynes, University of North Carolina sophomore

In her 1987 book, *Campus Life,* Helen Lefkowitz Horowitz, in chronicling the development of undergraduate culture on American campuses and universities since the end of the eighteenth century, notes in her concluding coda that the children of the rebels of the 1960s were now entering college. She predicted that they would bring with them to campus "an assertive independence" and "heightened consciences."[5] She foresaw a new brand of college rebel, a student who wants to learn, believes in academic accomplishment, but is free of the mindless grade chasing that characterized many of the students she observed in the 1980s. She predicted that these new rebels, the children of the old rebels of the sixties, would want things to change and would soon be "transcending the tired plots of the past to create new scenarios."

Her predictions have proved to be unfounded. Although one may find pockets of such students at places like Duke and Middlebury, they represent a minority. Many seem to believe that college life is merely a step on the way to law school or medical school, a necessary evil to be endured before Wall Street, even though few will actually end up there. They have come to college because they want power — power as defined in this society's conventional terms — not because they want to change their school or themselves. Why?

5. Helen Lefkowitz Horowitz, *Campus Life* (New York: Knopf, 1987), p. 290.

24

One of the main complaints of student leaders is that "students are far too passive." They confess to great frustration in their attempts to organize and mobilize students for common concerns. In a meeting with some of our most outstanding undergraduates, all recipients of major scholarships, many of them were quite critical of their experience in the university, yet none of them at the table that night had ever seriously considered running for any student government office. It was amazing that students would complain about the lack of social options, yet always saw this as a problem for the administration to solve, rather than as a specifically student problem begging for peculiarly student solutions.

Perhaps our students merely mirror the political apathy of the populace, the cynicism about political solutions to human problems. Perhaps prestigious, competitive universities draw a relatively high number of students who have been the beneficiaries (or victims?) of a high amount of parental care and initiative on their behalf.

A survey of 1994's first-year students showed that their interest in politics was at the lowest ebb in the entire twenty-nine-year history of the national freshman survey. While in 1966, the survey's first year, 57.8 percent said that "keeping up with political affairs" was very important for them, by 1994 that number had dropped to 31.9 percent.[6]

We find ourselves agreeing with Duke senior Evan Berg's contention that far more students ought to be asking themselves, "Are we really getting educated?" Part of faculty and administrative frustration with the current state of student life is related to student docility and the failure of students both to reflect critically upon their situation or to organize to change it.

Yet a student government representative asked, "When students take initiative, when they really do think in class and out of class, are they being rewarded? Students get the message that the best way to get ahead is to 'stick with the program,' to 'keep your head down,' and 'keep your nose to the grindstone' rather than to think. The way

---

6. "Disengaged Freshmen," *Chronicle of Higher Education,* January 13, 1995, p. A29.

the students perceive it, some of their most popular professors have been denied tenure and dismissed." It appears to the student on-looker that these people were "punished for their good teaching," but they are powerless to change the system.

"Patterns of passivity begin the freshman year," noted one student. "Freshmen are marginalized. During orientation, their main job is to sit and to be instructed. They are lectured to. If one is in the sciences, the impression of freshman year is very large classes which are exclusively lectures where nobody takes the trouble to know your name. This clashes with the 9:1 teacher ratio which is listed in the catalog."

Another agreed: "The marginalization continues. The University Writing Course (UWC) has become the most determinative academic experience of the freshman year. In the UWC, there are rigid rules for writing and freshmen must follow them. There is no interest in content, or ideas, just in one's ability to follow the rules."

The students felt they were not being considered in decisions about faculty. "Our job is to pay tuition so you can do your writing and research," charged a senior campus activist. "Students are only here as a necessary evil — to finance faculty research." These comments may be peculiar to life in a research university.

In some students' minds, all of this combines to produce a docile student body in which there is little acknowledgment of students as people with any control over their lives. Students are initiated into a system with certain norms, certain expectations. Because a student is here for only four years, because students have little knowledge of the history of the university, the university presents an eternal, God-ordained visage. "I guess it's always been like this here," was how one student responded to a question about academic life. The status quo appears to be divinely ordained, created this way for all the ages. Even among would-be student activists, the university appears to be a huge, amorphous blob of bureaucracy that is difficult to penetrate.

Student docility is a major theme of Paul Rogat Loeb's *A Generation at the Crossroads: Apathy and Action on the American Campus.* Loeb says we have taught this generation of students that

26

Societies change only through actions of people at the top, that notions of a greater common good are a mask for hypocrisy, that they should mistrust those who try to shape a better world. [American society] taught them that the best hope, for themselves and America, is to hunker down and do their best to adapt to whatever the powers that be happen to offer. It's not surprising that these students mostly place their faith in private dreams.[7]

Loeb believes the political disengagement of today's students is a reflection of today's society in general, particularly as that society is mirrored by the faculty. He quotes a Williams student who notes that "Armchair liberal professors create armchair liberal students."[8]

Bloom on Student Apathy

[T]he souls of young people are in a condition like that of the first men in the state of nature — spiritually unclad, unconnected, isolated, with no inherited or unconditional connection with anything or anyone. They can be anything they want to be, but they have no particular reason to want to be anything in particular.[9]

When a student arrives on campus, that student begins a subtle but well-developed program of initiation into a new culture that, like any culture, has a rather clear set of rigidly enforced values, myths, stories, and symbols, a history and a unique language.[10]

7. Paul Rogat Loeb, *A Generation at the Crossroads: Apathy and Action on the American Campus* (New Brunswick, N.J.: Rutgers University Press, 1994), p. 126.
8. Loeb, p. 94.
9. Allan Bloom, *The Closing of the American Mind* (New York: Simon and Schuster, 1987), p. 87.
10. See R. S. Peters, "Education as Initiation," in *Philosophical Analysis and*

Within the university, the administratively sanctioned "official culture" holds less sway over students' lives than that devised and sanctioned by the students themselves. Initiation into the student-sanctioned culture begins long before a student arrives as a first-year student. This student-sanctioned culture is a major part of what Lawrence Kohlberg has examined as "the hidden curriculum," that unstated yet powerful force on students' lives that is embedded in the institution as a whole.[11]

Campus image is an amorphous, subtle, but powerful force. There are campus norms that are difficult for a new student, who is anxious to "fit in," to break out of. These norms tell the students that, as far as their social life is concerned, it is "kegs or nothing."

In the 1960s, before Duke moved to a four-course load and abolished Saturday classes, the nickname for the campus was "The Gothic Rockpile." Now our students often refer to us as "The Gothic Wonderland." What does that change in self-designation say?

Student tours of campus, orientation, and conversations with high school friends who are already on campus are all factors in the initiation of a new student into the campus culture. When does a student begin to be initiated into the campus system?

An alumnus tells a prospective student, "You'll love it at State. I was in a fraternity. Everybody is in a fraternity there and we had a great time. Have you ever lived in the South? Well, at southern schools, fraternities are very important. You'll certainly want to join one when you arrive there." The prospective student is already picking up signals and clues about what life is like at the university.

Unfortunately, the memory of the alumnus may be somewhat blurred through the years about what actually goes on there. Also, fraternity life in the late 1950s may have been a very different experience from fraternity life in the mid-1990s. For instance, at Duke, where less than 40 percent of undergraduate men are now

Education, ed. Reginald D. Arenhambault (London: Routledge and Kegan Paul, 1965), pp. 87-111.

11. Lawrence Kohlberg, "The Moral Atmosphere of the School," *Readings in Moral Education,* pp. 149-63.

members of fraternities, some wonder if fraternity behavior is worse because contemporary fraternities lack the ameliorating influence of a wider array of members. They now confine themselves to the "hard-core" party animals. We do not know.

One of the strongest messages we received from interviews with a group of admissions officers was: "The university needs to decide what it wants to be. It is very difficult to recruit students into an entity which appears to have no idea of who it is. If the university can ever decide who it wants to be, we are confident that we can recruit students on that basis. Unfortunately, we receive many conflicting signals from present students, alumni, and the administration."

These conflicting signals often lead to a sense, on the part of many students, that they have been somehow deceived or misled in coming to the college. Groups of top scholarship recipients revealed a fairly high level of dissatisfaction with their experience. A number of them said things like "I think I was sold the wrong school." Rarely is their dissatisfaction with the faculty or with their classes. Rarely does it appear tied to specific policies of the university. It is more related to certain subtle, unstated aspects of the student ethos that they find confining, anti-intellectual. "Try bringing up a book you've read, or a great lecture you've just heard in class and other students will tell you, 'keep it in class. My brain meter's not running now.'"

We noted that "Sometimes, in fairness to the university, the university gives scholarships, not only to those people who represent who we are, but also to those who represent who we want to be."

Fair enough, said the students, but the university appears to do little, after an energetic and expensive recruiting process, to set up those structures and conditions whereby these "ideal students" can find a home within the present system. A notable exception is the "FOCUS" program at Duke in which a group of first-year students can elect to participate in a program their first year where they live together and have the majority of their classes together with the same professors in order to build community and to foster faculty-student interaction.

Many African-American students told us they had been elaborately entertained during our African-American student recruitment weekend. On the basis of that weekend, it appeared to them that the university was very "Afrocentric." However, when they got there, they found a different picture. This is what students sometimes refer to as the "viewbook syndrome." That is, there is a huge gap between the pictures of contented students sitting with professors under trees, or walking hand in hand with other students across campus, and the realities of what life is really like. Does this "viewbook syndrome" contribute to the fact that only about half of American students graduate from the institution in which they first enroll?

When new students arrive on our campus, they are guided by FACs (first-year advisers) and their RAs (residential advisers), who "show them the ropes." These students appear to be a more powerful influence on a student's first days here than any member of the faculty or administration.

Turning Off the Academic

In high school, I loved chemistry. But I had to hide. If I didn't, if I made the mistake of talking about chemistry with other students, I was labeled as a "geek." My mother kept telling me, "You're going to love college. In college, everybody will be just like you, have the same interest in being a good student that you have, love to sit up all night in the dormitory bull sessions discussing things." Unfortunately, that is not how it has been here. The same anti-intellectual remarks are made here. If you try to discuss something that happened in class, or something from your reading for class, they'll ridicule you. People want to be able to turn off the academic switch the minute they get out of class.

Duke University sophomore

A student talked about her first day at the university. After a heady day of presentations, and more presentations on various aspects of university life, her FAC led a group of them back across campus toward the dorm. On the way to the dorm he said, "Let me show you something wonderful."

They took a detour by the parking lot. There, in the parking lot, they all were made to stare at his new car.

"Would you like to sit in it?" he asked. "Would you like to start the engine?"

As they were standing there, one freshman woman leaned over to her friend and said, "This is depressing. He is the person I thought I had left behind in high school."

Students do not walk into a vacuum when they arrive as new members of the university community. They are subtly but powerfully initiated into a distinct culture — a culture that mitigates against serious and sustained intellectual engagement by the students.

The "We work hard, we play hard" mentality thus fosters a rather rowdy, carefree, anti-intellectual image of the "perfect" college student. Seen in its best light, this means that students are known for their exuberance, their enthusiasm at sports events, and their general love of life. At its worst, it means that our students are engaged in activities that not only do not contribute to the academic mission of the university but actually work against that mission by trivializing the time they spend here.

Many undergraduate colleges appear to have structured themselves on some version of the traditional English (Oxford, Cambridge) system of educating the upper class.[12] Sons and daughters of the economically elite, who may have already had a rigorous education before coming to college, are allowed to drift through the college at their own discretion. Already economically secure, they need not bother themselves over their prospects for employment

12. The notion that higher education ought to be enjoyed for its own sake, as a pleasant pastime of the upper classes with adequate leisure, is perhaps best articulated in Thorstein Veblen, *The Higher Learning in America: A Memorandum on the Conduct of Universities by Businessmen* (New York: B. W. Huebsch, 1918).

after college — the family fortune awaits them. *Brideshead Revisited*, quoted at the beginning of this chapter, is an image of this relaxed, patrician form of student life.

Transposing this form of undergraduate life upon middle- and lower-middle-class American students, offering them a great amount of free time, allowing them to drift through their four or more years at the university, graduating with no particular sense of direction or competence to support themselves, seems to us peculiarly inappropriate. When there is no family fortune awaiting these aimless wanderers at the end of their undergraduate years, they are apt to feel terribly deceived.[13] Surely the large amount of poorly used free time enjoyed by many students is one of the causes for alcohol abuse rather than merely its symptom. The Califano report noted that binge drinking (five or more drinks at one time) is about 20 percent higher among college students than among their noncollege counterparts. Students at privately owned institutions tend to binge-drink more than those who attend public colleges and universities (48 percent versus 39 percent).

Thus one administrator stated flatly, "Reinstitute Saturday classes and add more early morning classes and you will not have a drinking problem on campus." When asked why Saturday and early-morning classes would not be reinstituted, the same administrator said, "Because the *faculty* would never agree to it; they love their free Saturdays more than the students."

University of Vermont undergraduates demonstrate such a lack of respect for the faculty that the School of Business faculty passed a resolution requiring that a copy of the "Classroom Protocol" be attached to each undergraduate course syllabus and be distributed to students.

---

13. Suzanne Littwin documents this tendency vividly in *The Postponed Generation: Why America's Grown-Up Kids Are Growing Up Later* (New York: Morrow, 1986).

UNIVERSITY OF VERMONT
CLASSROOM PROTOCOL

1. Students are expected to attend and be prepared for ALL regularly scheduled classes.

2. Students are expected to arrive on time and stay in class until the class period ends. If a student knows in advance that s/he will need to leave early, s/he should notify the instructor before the class period begins.

3. Students are expected to treat faculty and fellow students with respect. For example, students must not disrupt class by leaving and reentering during class, must not distract class by making noise, and must be attentive to comments being made by the instructor and by peers.

4. Food is not allowed in classrooms. Beverages are permissible at the instructor's discretion.

5. Instructors will inform students of any special/additional class expectations.

Most students, it seems, believe "academic" applies only to what one does in a classroom a few hours per week. Ironically, many of us faculty have the same perception, taking little responsibility for anything that goes on outside the classroom. Of course, few faculty are seen on campus after class hours anyway. Faculty and students share a disjointed, limited view of "academic."

After class the students are left to the "student-life administrators," a new class of university professional that takes care of all aspects of "student life." Few of these administrators were once faculty members. Rather, they are professional student-care-givers, addressing students' needs, and are reluctant to pass judgment upon the students, since to do so might infringe on the students' "freedom" or compromise "diversity" on campus. At most campuses, it is clear that these student administrators, precisely because they are not faculty, have little direct power to influence campus life in fundamental ways.[14]

The faculty attend to the students' brains; in all other areas of their lives, students are left to their own devices. Faculty would do well to ponder questions like: What conditions shaped your own intellectual development? Who changed you and how?

A first-year student from a small town in North Carolina spoke of himself as "floating" since his arrival at Duke, not really being engaged by his studies. One night a popular professor spent four hours in his dormitory commons discussing various matters, particularly race relations in America. The professor was African-American, unlike most of the students. When the new student asserted that he had overcome his earlier racist feelings and was able to accept black people, the professor challenged him by asking him who his three best friends were on campus. Whom did he go to the beach with over fall break?

"It really hit me," said the student. "My actions did not match my ideals. I decided that I wanted more of an education than I was getting. I therefore intentionally went out and made contact with a couple of black students. I am determined to overcome my past."

Such is the potential of personal interaction between faculty and students. Enlightenment notions of education have conditioned us to step back from ideas, viewing them and those who hold them "objectively." Thus we turn specifics into generalities and particularities into abstractions.

---

14. "[T]he pressures felt by junior faculty have diminished faculty involvement in both the formulation and the implementation of student conduct policies. . . . the growing size and complexity of university administration in the period after World War II, . . . has contributed both to fragmentation and specialization among administrators and to a general sense of distance between faculty and administration. . . . Relatively few senior academic administrators besides deans of students, and even fewer faculty members, now take an active interest in discipline. . . . Thus the ironic and unintended result of higher standards and expectations for student-affairs personnel has been the erosion of any sense of shared responsibility for matters of student conduct." David A. Hoekema, *Campus Rules and Moral Community: In Place of In Loco Parentis* (Lanham, Md.: Rowman & Littlefield Pub., 1994), p. 145.

We must teach students not to step back from ideas but to step into ideas, to wrestle with them through intense encounters with others. Aristotle believed that it was impossible to teach anything important to people who are not your friends. Only friends know how to hurt you in the right way. Yet the modern university appears to organize itself in such a way that faculty and students will rarely interact with one another in such a way as to become friends. The faculty go their way, absorbed in the research that will determine their professional future; the students go their way, blending into a student culture that is ruthless in enforcing its values and mores. About the best we can hope for is satisfied customers rather than honest and open friends.

Thus the Califano report says alcohol abuse on campus will not change until there is a concerted effort to change the campus culture. Change of culture is not impossible. Consider the changes in our culture's perception of and use of cigarettes. The Califano report says, in regard to alcohol, that colleges and universities must "Shift the college culture away from accepting alcohol abuse and its con-sequences as part of the 'rites of passage.' To do this, institutions need to develop a collective, comprehensive strategy that begins with a clearly articulated statement of values and is supported by sustained public discussion and the commitment of resources." They must then "Reverse the image of alcohol from a liberating to a debilitating force through increased education and awareness and counter advertising. Abusing alcohol must be recognized as a crutch to deal with stress and to cope with transition" (p. 6).[15]

Yet a "clearly articulated statement of values" is precisely what many of our educational institutions lack. More than that, too many colleges and universities lack the conviction that our students are a talented, valuable trust that deserves the highest expectations from us. We lack confidence that the student years are a privileged time and space apart to reflect and to grow; that there is important work to be done during these years; and that the life of the mind is an adventure that requires not just the payment of tuition but hard, consistent, disciplined thought.

15. As reported in *The New York Times*, June 11, 1994, p. 21.

When one of our sons began high school at a boarding school in the mountains of North Carolina, the headmaster of the school, speaking to the parents of the new students, remarked that "To our knowledge, alcohol has no educational purpose. The purpose of this school is education. Therefore, alcohol has no place on this campus and the use of alcohol by our students is forbidden."

What struck us about the headmaster's statement was that it was not only painfully obvious but, alas, all too rare. Forget the moral issues related to alcohol abuse. The educational issues alone are pervasive. More educators need to stand before their students *as educators,* to regard them not as consumers or customers but *as students,* to judge all college activities on the basis of their educational value, to reaffirm that the main "business" of a college is education.

When our former president, a psychiatrist, addressed incoming freshmen (oops, "first-year students"; the term *freshman* has been deemed exclusive and demeaning by our campus keepers of words), he mentioned campus social issues like acquaintance rape, racism, and homophobia. He told them, "As a psychiatrist, I look at these issues in this way." Then he gave them a few psychiatric insights into these social issues.

When our current president, a political scientist, gave her first-year student address, she said, "As a political scientist, I believe that . . . ," and then she proceeded to apply her insights as a political scientist to the challenges of their first year at Duke. This is exactly the sort of thing that we think ought to distinguish administrators in higher education. They ought to be people who are formed — *disciplined* — by their respective disciplines, people who embody the insights and practices of their intellectual craft. By their words and acts, they ought to demonstrate to the students how these intellectual perspectives enable one to deal with the world.

We long to make alcohol abuse an intellectual issue.

Tradition on the Wane: College Drinking

Even though abusive drinking has been a focus of increased public attention and campus counseling because of its links with hazing injuries and date rapes, college officials and health experts who follow student drinking agree in several recent studies that the number of college-age drinkers has in fact been declining for two decades.

One in four students reported abstaining even from an occasional beer in 1971; today it is nearly half, according to a recent survey of more than 300,000 students nationwide by the University of California at Los Angeles. The average consumption for those who do drink regularly has dropped to about 13 drinks a week, down from 14.3 in 1982, according to another national study, with much of the overall decline attributed to light to moderate drinkers, who now have 6 drinks a week, down from 8.4.

Among the drinkers, however, binge drinking remains intractable, all the studies suggest.[16]

We work hard, we play hard. But *thinking* hard requires a complex system of interaction between generations, engagement, patience, linkage of ideas and experiences, time, and space. On the modern campus, sometimes the student's self-congratulatory claim to play hard and to work hard is an escape from the more demanding process of thinking hard.

16. "Tradition on the Wane: College Drinking," *New York Times*, February 5, 1995.

CHAPTER 3

Teach Me How to Be a Moneymaking Machine

Modern man has transformed himself into a commodity; he experiences his life energy as an investment with which he should make the highest profit, considering his position and the situation on the personality market. He is alienated from himself, from his fellow men, and from nature. His main aim is profitable exchange of his skills, knowledge, and of himself, his "personality package" with others who are equally intent on a fair and profitable exchange. Life has no goal except the one to move, no principle except the one of fair exchange, no satisfaction except the one to consume.[1]

For several years, students in our School of Business were asked to write a personal strategic plan for the ten-year period after their graduation. The question posed to them was, "What do you want to be when you grow up?" With few exceptions, they wanted three things — money, power, and things (very big things, including vacation homes, expensive foreign automobiles, yachts, and even airplanes). Primarily concerned with their careers and the growth of

1. Erich Fromm, *The Art of Loving* (New York: Perennial, 1974), p. 88.

38

their financial portfolios, their personal plans contained little room for family, intellectual development, spiritual growth, or social responsibility.

Their mandate to the faculty was, "Teach me how to be a moneymaking machine." "Give me only the facts, tools, and techniques required to ensure my instantaneous financial success." All else was irrelevant.

Careerism is by no means limited to schools of business; it is as pervasive throughout colleges and universities as the work hard–play hard ethos. On the surface, a preoccupation with getting the right first job or getting into the best possible law school, medical school, or graduate school might appear to be a contradiction of the work hard–play hard philosophy. It is not.

When students do work hard, it is often to get the grades necessary to achieve their narrowly defined vocational or professional objectives, not because they have an abiding intellectual interest in the courses themselves. The prevailing attitude of many of our students — and more particularly their parents — is that they are paying $25,000 a year to be here, and they expect a high return on their investment, namely, access to the professional schools of their choice. Preprofessionalism is another important force contributing to grade inflation.

As the North American economy is transposed from a manufacturing economy into a service economy, a college degree is perceived as more important in providing access to the better jobs. The earnings gap between those who have degrees, even associate degrees, and those who do not has increased by 20 percentage points in the last decade. Thus the rise in college enrollments over the last decade.

Paradoxically, students are finding that they face an uncertain economic future. The numbers cited in a *Wall Street Journal* article entitled "Generation X" were disconcerting.[2] One in three nineties' graduates will take jobs that don't require a sheepskin, says the Bureau of Labor. They call it "McJob." Only 20 percent of today's

2. "Generation X," *Wall Street Journal,* July 28, 1993.

graduates believe they will achieve the "good life" as defined by their parents and Ronald Reagan — down from 43 percent just nine years ago (Roper Organization report). New York labor economist Audrey Freedman says, "this generation of grads knows that permanence and stability are not achievable anymore." Reality bites. Corporate America calls it "downsizing," they call it a stripped-down two-door Toyota.

Reality Bites

So my sister graduated from Brown. She was always the intellectual in the family. She made great grades, did all the work. So where is she now, two years after her graduation? She's on the living room sofa, expert on soap operas. She's looked for a job. Waitress was the best thing she could find.

So, you could say that I'm scared. You see your smart sister on the sofa for a couple of years after college, it will do something to you.

Duke University sophomore

One quickly learns on today's campus not to ask seniors, "What will you be doing in June?"

The undergraduate's fear of a shrinking job market is driving the curriculum in interesting ways. When our School of Business discontinued its undergraduate course offerings several years ago so as to concentrate on its popular MBA program, the sociology department quickly moved to fill the vacuum created by the business school's retreat from undergraduate education. Because of declining enrollments in the 1980s, sociology was a serious candidate for divestiture. The department began introducing courses in marketing, organizational development, and the sociology of markets and offered its majors the option of a certificate of management. For undergraduates planning to pursue an MBA after graduation or a career in corporate America, this program was a big hit, and the sociology department was saved from extinction.

One of the most important gods of today's college students is technology — particularly the personal computer (PC). Computers are used for entertainment, word processing, and scientific calculations. Students are mesmerized by the silent hum of a smoothly running machine that gives them the illusion that they can control their own destiny and deny their mortality. So-called knowledge-based technology represents the ultimate solution to all of their problems — professional, financial, technical, social, political, and even geopolitical. Colleges compete on the basis of the number of PCs available per student and brag about being a "connected campus" — each room has its own computer linkup. The advantages of "interactive communication" are pushed on campus, the brave new world where people talk to one another via modem.

Participants in the Pew Higher Education Roundtable laud the value of this technologically induced interaction:

> The interactive power of telecommunications is opening the way to different means not just of conveying information but of responding to questions that arise in the natural course of learning. The concept of "classroom time" can come to seem a quaint anachronism when considered against the ability of the proposed information superhighway to lead students to sources of information. . . . The results can be improved student mentoring as well as an enriched form of Socratic inquiry. . . . What telemarketing and phone banks did for catalog sales, what QVC did for home shopping . . . the information highway is about to do for distance learning and higher education.[3]

3. "Policy Perspectives," *Pew Higher Education Roundtable*, April 1994, vol. 5, no. 3, sec. A.

The Pew Roundtable participants then worry about what might happen to higher education if new, exclusively technologically based companies enter the education market and take over the education that has been the monopoly of colleges and universities.

We believe that much education may be done better by technology. Why shouldn't creative software companies become the educators of persons preparing for jobs that mainly require the accumulation and assimilation of data? Perhaps this would free colleges from their attempts to be all things to all people. The line between technical schools and colleges could be more sharply drawn, and colleges and universities might again discover the one, absolutely essential ingredient in higher education — a face-to-face engagement of the teacher with the student as they pursue matters more significant than the accumulation and arrangement of data.

We wonder if the academy's current infatuation with its new technology is disconnecting us. It has been said that every advance in technology tends to increase time, decrease space, and destroy community. Computers enable us to crunch vast amounts of data in a split second and communicate with scholars around the world in an instant, but we do so without leaving the confines of our computer screen. Sitting alone in their rooms, gazing at their computers, having random e-mail interactions with some student at the other side of the continent, the student on the technologically "connected campus" is encountering much loneliness and isolation. Surfing on the Internet until 4:00 A.M. is rarely of educational benefit. "It's Nintendo for nineteen-year-olds," said one honest undergraduate.

But why should we be surprised that alcohol abuse, careerism, and an obsession with high technology pervade college campuses whose administrators and faculty boast of being value-neutral? In such a passive, live-and-let-live environment the marketplace is a more important force in shaping the moral character of students than is the faculty. Courses on professional ethics and social responsibility are few, not only in liberal arts colleges but also in law schools and medical schools.

What Is the Most Important
Lesson to Be Taught?

Throughout most of its history, American higher education has understood its social mission to include instruction in fundamental ethical values. While early childhood experience, family, church, and precollegiate education are certainly key factors . . . Late adolescence and early adulthood can be equally formative periods in shaping moral predispositions.

It is during these years — at exactly the time of the four-year undergraduate experience — that important opportunities exist for the cultivation of responsibility, justice, and compassion. It is during these years that a sense of the common good . . . can be nurtured.

Young men and women do change and grow morally during their college years. How they change, and in what direction, will be influenced by the intellectual and the social environment college provides for them. Colleges and universities in the United States today must focus anew on their role as teachers of value, judgement, and character.[4]

A University of Virginia administrator, when asked about alcohol abuse on that campus, proudly proclaimed, "Our school has no opinion on alcohol."

"No opinion?" we asked.

"Absolutely. If we had an opinion about alcohol, if we made

4. Bruce Jennings, executive director of the Hastings Center, quoted in the *Chronicle of Higher Education,* January 13, 1995, p. B3. One of the best extended discussions of the moral purposes of higher education is Edward LeRoy Long, Jr., *Higher Education as a Moral Enterprise* (Washington, D.C.: Georgetown University Press, 1992).

some public statement about it to our students, that could leave us open to litigation, would increase our liability. Therefore, if students drink or don't drink, we have no opinion about the matter."

The thought that a university, a place presumed to be bubbling with "opinions," prided itself on steadfastly refusing to have an opinion struck us as strange.

The Recommendation

I believe that one product of our allegedly value-neutral environment was Ricardo, a bright, aggressive, angry young man, who was once arrested for his involvement in one of the more violent drunken campus brawls. A couple of years later, Ricardo wrote to me requesting a letter of recommendation in support of his application to law school. He apparently assumed I was unaware of his encounter with the campus police. He was mistaken. I told him that I would be willing to write a recommendation for him provided that he met three conditions. First, I wanted a copy of the student newspaper account of the violent campus episode in which he had been involved. Second, I wanted an official explanation from the university indicating how the matter had been adjudicated. Third, I wanted him to write me a letter explaining why he thought he could become a good lawyer, given his behavior at the university. I never heard from Ricardo again.

Tom Naylor

Intimidated by the slim prospect that wisdom will be gained at the university, we content ourselves with the mere acquisition of "values," or the collection of interesting "ideas." Fearful of the fracturing debate that might ensue if we challenged our students' goals and ethics, we opt instead for the fractured "diversity" of the modern campus, diversity that too often translates into "you stay out of my life and I will stay out of yours."

The Making of a Math Major

I've made a decision. I'm going to major in mathematics. Sure, I liked economics and did well in my first economics courses. But in three courses in that department, I never had a professor who offered me one word of encouragement, or even criticism. I'm sorry, I just can't learn like that. I had one professor who came to class every day with the attitude, "Well, there you are, damnit. So let me get through this lecture and then I can get back to my research." She was a consultant for a bunch of big companies so she was gone a lot of the time. Anyway, I've decided to go to math because I've met a professor there who has really shown some interest in me.[5]

Junior math major

Knowledge is not a matter of the technologically aided accumulation of information, of the collection of more data. Skills of discernment must be acquired. Judgments about the information cannot be endlessly deferred. Yet critical discernment and judgment are precisely the virtues of which modern higher education is terrified.

Thus, in his 1993 inaugural address, the president of the University of Vermont defines the purpose of that university as "First

5. In 1989 the Carnegie Foundation noted that 50 percent of the students felt like a number on campus. Seventy-five percent reported that no faculty member knew them by name. Reported in *The Chronicle of Higher Education*, April 14, 1995.

and foremost an institution engaged in the discovery and dissemination of knowledge, dedicated to the integration of scholarship, research, and service. We exist for the purpose of the advancement of humankind through the rigorous and relentless pursuit of truth in our classrooms and in our laboratories. We are a place where knowledge is created and taught."

Aside from the rather easy linkage of knowledge with truth, there is also the troubling impression, in the president's remarks, that universities are here mainly to produce, store, and transport some commodity called "knowledge." A capitalist culture has a way of commodifying everything, even knowledge. Like some vast, very expensive yet inefficient computer, the university and its inhabitants crunch data without presuming to judge the quality, usefulness, or value of the data. Every institution in our society is valued in terms of productivity, so now the university produces knowledge.

Catholic scholar Bernard Lonergan wrote fifty years ago (in language dated by its gender exclusivity),

> New books pour forth annually by the thousands; our libraries need ever more space. But the vast modern effort to understand meaning in all its manifestations has not been matched by a comparable effort in judging meaning. The effort to understand is the common task of unnumbered scientists and scholars. But judging and deciding are left to the individual, and he finds his plight desperate. There is far too much to be learnt before he could begin to judge. Yet judge he must and decide he must if he is to exist, if he is to be a man.[6]

Values must not only be "clarified," they must be debated, judged, exemplified, demonstrated, and tested before the young if they are to be embraced by and inculcated in the young. Although

6. Bernard J. F. Lonergan, "Cognitional Structure," in *Collection,* ed. F. E. Crowe (New York: Herder and Herder, 1967), p. 235.

they have made a rather limp list of mere questions about values, we applaud the movement toward reconsideration of such matters that is advocated by the Wingspread Group:

Taking Values Seriously

- How does our educational program match the claims of our recruiting brochures, and where is it falling short?
- How does our core curriculum of required courses respond to the needs of our students for a rigorous liberal education enabling them to "live rightly and well in a free society"? Where does it fall short?
- In what ways does our institution model the values and skills expected in our community? Where and how are we falling short? ⟨ *our clients*
- What steps might we take to improve the general climate of civility on our campus?
- How comprehensive and effective is the code of professional conduct and ethics for our faculty and staff? When was it last reviewed?
- On what ways does our institution and its educational program promote the development of shared values, specifically the civic virtues listed below, among our students?
  - respect for the individual and commitment to equal opportunity in a diverse society;
  - the belief that our common interests exceed our individual differences;
  - support for the freedoms enunciated in the Bill of Rights, including freedom of religion, of the press, of speech, and the right to assemble;
  - the belief that individual rights and privileges are accompanied by responsibilities to others;
  - respect for the views of others; and

47

- the conviction that no one is above the law.
- What moral and ethical questions should we be putting to the student groups and organizations we sanction on campus? What standards of conduct do we expect of these groups? How have we made these standards clear?
- How do the activities of our athletic programs square with our institution's stated values, and where do they fall short?
- What steps will we take to assure that next year's entering students will graduate as individuals of character more sensitive to the needs of community, more competent to contribute to society, more civil in their habits of thought, speech, and action?
- What other related questions should we address at our institution?[7]

Perhaps there is a more positive reading on the careerism and preprofessionalism of today's students. Faced with decades of unrelenting tuition increases, more students and their parents are asking, "What are we getting for our money?" With an increase in the number of second-career students who are exclusively paying their own way through college, this question gains urgency. While faculty and administrators may deplore this "consumer mentality" among our students, it is unwise for faculty and administrators who have asked students to go into considerable debt and to make major financial sacrifice to criticize students for asking, "Is college worth the sacrifice?"

Part of the public's anger against higher education is directed at faculties who appear to be a kind of economically privileged class that has forgotten its responsibility to serve the larger social order. Today's

7. Report of the Wingspread Group on Higher Education, *An American Imperative: Higher Expectations for Higher Education* (Racine, Wis.: Johnson Foundation, 1993), p. 29.

faculty appears, to the general public, like a self-perpetuating oligarchy that demonstrates a patrician disdain for the opinions of anyone outside the academic establishment and whose only responsibility to the students is the hope that, through their teaching, they might produce a few clones of themselves. Faculty salaries may be much better than the salaries of their constituency. Faculty enjoy a much greater degree of job security and a virtual absence of accountability, particularly external accountability. Higher education appears to many to be utterly impervious to serious change in its self-protective practices. Now, to add insult to injury, academia (including the authors of this book!) contemptuously refers to the ugly "careerism," "grim preprofessionalism," and "consumerism" of its students!

Are we being fair to the modern campus in these characterizations? Certainly, a number of significant positive trends evidence concern and action among our students. At Duke and elsewhere, student volunteerism has become an important part of student life. Each week, 1,700 Duke students, close to 20 percent of our student body, give at least two hours of volunteer work to the community. The tutoring program, which trains and places Duke student tutors in the Durham schools, is a model of student activism.

In a survey of the nation's new college students, the annual Freshmen Survey, the most popular social issue was the environment. Eighty-four percent of the nation's freshmen favor greater efforts to protect the environment.[8] Yet this same statistic, reported in the *Chronicle of Higher Education,* was found in an article entitled "Disengaged Freshmen," an article showing that political engagement and social concern among this year's freshmen were at the lowest ebb in nearly thirty years.

The burning issues of the day on most college campuses have little to do with political philosophy, religion, ethics, or social responsibility but rather more to do with consumer issues of campus food service, class scheduling, restrictions imposed on student social life, and recruiting by prospective employers. Of course, to be fair,

8. "Disengaged Freshmen," *Chronicle of Higher Education,* January 13, 1995, p. A29.

the hottest concerns of most faculty are salaries, benefits, job security, parking, and turf protection. Thus, when faculty complain about the vacuousness of student intellectual life, it may be a case of, in the words of Pogo, "We have met the enemy and he is us."

Now we may have hit at the heart of the matter. Now we see why faculty are so reluctant to argue about the values and the behavior of students. If we push our students in these areas, our students might react by challenging us. Questioned about the use of their time, students might turn and question us faculty on the use of our time. Chided for their zealous pursuit of material acquisitions, they might inquire into the nature of our vacations, job benefits, and salaries. And then where would we be?

Alcohol Abuse on Campus

"Alcohol abuse on campus? Are you talking about alcohol abuse among students or among faculty?"

"I'm talking about alcohol abuse among students, of course. Why do you ask about faculty?"

"Well, I've got this professor who is clearly an alcoholic. I should know. My dad's been one for a long time. I know the signs. This guy never meets a class on Mondays. He's always 'sick' then. He also uses this really heavy breath spray of some kind. I'm sure he's got a drinking problem. But it doesn't seem to hurt him on the faculty."

"Now I think I remember why we faculty are not going to push you students too hard on the subject of alcohol abuse!"

Conversation between Will and a college sophomore

Walker Percy once characterized modern, mechanical humanity as the "living dead," "people who seem to be living lives which are

50

good by all sociological standards," but who "somehow seem to be more dead than alive."[9] Percy's novels are full of bright, urbane, educated folk who, having assured all of their creature comforts, assume that they have risen above their creaturely status, that they are now fully human. Yet, to use an image of Adam Smith, we may have constructed for ourselves a sort of gilded cage, a plush trap of our own devising. Our creature comforts give us the illusion of life, yet we are trapped in our own devices. What would it take for us to break free, to lay hold of our lives with intelligence and courage?

Are we reaping the results of a generation of students abandoned by the previous generation, left to their own devices, having no more textured goal for their lives than to be rendered into efficient, passive machines for the acquisition of money?[10]

We noted how some schools fear the threat of liability and use this as an excuse for not intruding into the lives of their students. In most court cases against institutions of higher education, the courts have ruled that colleges do not have an inherent responsibility to protect and to control their students. Colleges are not *in loco parentis*, in place of parents in their students' lives. We have been maneuvered into a philosophy that David Hoekema mockingly characterizes as *non sum mater tua* ("I'm not your mama").[11]

However, in a 1991 case against the University of Delaware, the court did establish that while universities cannot control their students, they do have "a duty to care." It strikes us as poignant that a court of law must remind a university that, in regard to its students, it has a duty to care. A college cannot be a parent, cannot hermetically seal its students from all of the pitfalls and foolishness of youth. But a college does have a duty to care.

---

9. Walker Percy, *Signposts in a Strange Land* (New York: Farrar, Straus and Giroux, 1991), p. 162.

10. Neil Howe and William Strauss attribute much of this student generation's emphasis on careerism to their having been raised in a time of high divorce rates and family instability. Divorce rates doubled between 1965 and 1975, just in time for the birth of today's undergraduates. *13th-GEN* (New York: Vintage Books, 1993).

11. David A. Hoekema, *Campus Rules and Moral Community: In Place of In Loco Parentis* (Lanham, Md.: Rowman & Littlefield Pub., 1994), p. 140.

THE PROBLEMS

CHAPTER 4

Meaninglessness

The function of education, . . . is to teach one to think intensively and to think critically. But education which stops with efficiency may prove the greatest menace to society. The most dangerous criminal may be the man gifted with reason but no morals. We must remember that intelligence is not enough. Intelligence plus character — that is the goal of true education. The complete education gives one not only power of concentration but worthy objectives upon which to concentrate.

. . . We must work passionately and indefatigably to bridge the gulf between our scientific progress and our moral progress. One of the great problems of mankind is that we suffer from a poverty of the spirit which stands in glaring contrast to our scientific and technological abundance. The richer we have become materially the poorer we have become morally and spiritually.[1]

When we began examining the crisis in higher education, we proceeded as if what were needed was more information on student life, more data. The belief that all human problems are the

1. Martin Luther King, Jr., *The Words of Martin Luther King, Jr.*, selected by Coretta Scott King (New York: Newmarket Press, 1983).

result of a lack of information typifies the technological understanding of life that Neil Postman calls "Technopoly." We now believe that insufficient information is not the problem.

Thomas Jefferson felt that, if information were made available to students, they would democratically sift through it and organize it themselves, knowing instinctively what to do with the information they had received through education. Jefferson believed that ideas were so ordered that students could make sense of what they heard and read and, by reason, judge its value and apply it to their lives. It is clear, in reading Jefferson on education, that he assumed a community of shared virtues and practices upon which education built.

Neil Postman argues persuasively that today we live in the aftermath of an age in which the connection "between information and human purpose has been severed, i.e., information appears indiscriminately, directed at no one in particular, in enormous volume and at high speeds, and disconnected from theory, meaning, or purpose." In the postmodern world we are learning that, in a sense, theory precedes information. We receive the information we are looking for. Our theory about what facts are important determines what facts we find. Today we understand what Jefferson did not — the character of the knower intrudes powerfully upon the nature of what is known. There is no way to have education without concern for the character of the educators.

Postman says that "any educational institution, if it is to function well in the management of information, must have a theory about its purpose and meaning, must have the means to give clear expression to its theory, and must do so, to a large extent, by excluding information."[2]

Lacking any definable ends, we are left only with means. Hoping to avoid moral judgments, we make only practical ones. University administration becomes adjudicating between conflicting entitlement claims, servicing an environment in which the student, unformed and uninformed in the purposes and ends of higher ed-

2. Neil Postman, *Technopoly: The Surrender of Culture to Technology* (New York: Knopf, 1992), p. 75.

ucation, is king. What we call "curriculum" is more a cafeteria line of subjects, a hodgepodge that lacks a clear vision of what constitutes an educated person. The image of personhood engendered by the curriculum appears to be that a person is someone without a point of view, devoid of commitment, but someone who has been exposed to the maximum number of lifestyle options.

Postman recalls Plato's *Phaedrus,* the legend of Thamus, in which Socrates complains about students who "will receive a quantity of information without proper instruction, and in consequence be thought very knowledgeable when they are for the most part quite ignorant. And because they are filled with the conceit of wisdom instead of real wisdom they will be a burden to society."[3]

What Postman seems to be saying is that colleges and universities have lost their way — administrators, faculty, and students. Administrators and faculty have no clearly defined vision of the future. Students have little idea who they are or what they want to be when they grow up. Waiting for the data to come in, we are frozen in indecision.[4] The specter of meaninglessness looms over the academy.

What Does It All Add Up To?

So you get here and they start asking you, "What do you think you want to major in?" "Have you thought about

---

3. Plato, *Phaedrus and Letters VII and VIII* (New York: Penguin Books, 1973), p. 96.

4. In analyzing the political apathy on campuses, Paul Rogat Loeb noted the paralyzing tendencies of "information overload": "Too many cable channels. Too many crises. Too many authorities with competing, clashing claims," which make students reluctant to take responsibility for the future. Paul Rogat Loeb, *A Generation at the Crossroads: Apathy and Action on the American Campus* (New Brunswick, N.J.: Rutgers University Press, 1994), p. 36.

Will remembers hearing then–campus activist minister William Sloane Coffin speaking contemptuously of the academic who "managed to see all sides of every issue, so carefully qualifying himself, that he never came down on any side." The acquisition of more data, increased information on a problem, does not lead to a solution to the problem.

what courses you want to take?" And you get the impression that's what it's all about — courses, majors. So you take the courses. You get your card punched. You try a little this and a little that. Then comes GRADUATION. And you wake up and you look at this bunch of courses and then it hits you: They don't add up to anything. It's just a bunch of courses. It doesn't mean a thing.

University of Michigan senior

What is missing in most colleges and universities is a well-defined sense of direction for administrators and faculty alike that goes beyond vague platitudes about teaching, research, and good citizenship. Why does the institution exist in the first place? Who are its constituents? What is it trying to accomplish?

We Sincerely Hope You Will Turn Out All Right

The typical college . . . proclaims its lofty goal of building responsible citizens and nurturing the sense of moral and social accountability only in the first few pages of the catalog, while its actions carry another message . . . [which] might be summarized thus: "We have excellent scholars for our faculty, maintain a good library, and fill the flower beds for parents' weekend; and we sincerely hope that the students will turn out all right."[5]

5. David A. Hoekema, *Campus Rules and Moral Community: In Place of* In Loco Parentis (Lanham, Md.: Rowman & Littlefield Pub., 1994), pp. 126-27.

A step forward out of this morass of indecision and indifference toward a frank consideration of the sort of people we are creating in higher education may begin with a statement of purpose. We believe it is important to communicate the institution's sense of purpose, values, and ethical principles to its trustees, administrators, faculty, students, nonacademic employees, alumni, and the public. A formal statement of the college or university's philosophy of education provides a compass for the institution.

An *educational philosophy* is concerned with the fundamental principles on which the affairs of a college or university are based. It should capture the sense of meaning and direction of the administration and faculty. A well-thought-out philosophy of education will have significant impact on the institution's goals, objectives, strategies, and policies as well as the administrative style, campus culture, and social environment. The educational philosophy is the heart and soul of the academy. It should provide a clear signal to administrators, faculty, nonteaching staff, students, and prospective students as to what the academy is all about. Perhaps it is better to speak of this statement as a statement of our mission rather than our philosophy in order to indicate that it is to receive embodiment in all of the activities of the school. It is first something that is said in order to be something that is then done.

We are hardly surprised that college administrators are so easily jerked around by students, alumni, and contributors. Academic administrators and faculty who have no well-defined sense of direction in their own personal lives have difficulty motivating students to climb on board a leaderless ship.

Lacking a theory of our life together in the academy, any statement of purpose or mission, we have become consumer-driven. Whatever student consumers want, whatever they think makes them happy, it is our duty to give. At Duke, Auxiliary Services (dining halls, snack bars, bookstores, etc.) has become the main focus of our administrative interaction with students; indeed, the whole university becomes but various aspects of Auxiliary Services — servicing ever more demanding student consumers. We prepare people to mirror their surrounding culture rather than to be visionary leaders in shaping that culture.

Members of the Pew Roundtable noted that, when the media turn their attention to American higher education, "Their dominant perspective is one of lumbering obsolescence; to them colleges and universities are dinosaurs trapped in the tar pits of political correctness and inefficient as well as self-serving attitudes and practices. The media's characterization of higher education is increasingly one of an industry that is exhausting itself in the attempt to escape from a morass of its own making. It is a view of colleges and universities as places that consume rather than produce energy."[6]

While media characterizations of anything, including higher education, are suspect, higher education is producing a growing number of internal critics. When Reynolds Price chastised both faculty and students, he said, "All of us, in long collusion, have failed to exert a sustained and serious attempt to nurture the literal heart of a great university." For Price, that "heart" consists of "an environment that is continuously encouraging to the more or less constant discussion of serious matters" and "an atmosphere that awards itself a steady supply of human beings (students, faculty, and other staff) who are fitted to converse with one another on serious matters or are willing to learn how."

Lack of information is not our problem. Our problem is that we have tried to have a university without arguing about what a university is, what we want out of ourselves, who we expect our students to grow up to be, what we expect them to give to the world. We thought we could educate in the absence of consensus, or even arguments about consensus. James B. Duke was quite clear that the only reason he could think of for a university was to produce people who would influence the world for good. Examine the founding documents of most of our colleges and universities and you will find similar statements. We should spend more time thinking about what is the best possible way to live in this community, and then we should unashamedly ask students to conform to the best way.

There is no way for us to sidestep the necessity of theory, the

6. "Policy Perspectives," *Pew Higher Education Roundtable*, April 1994, vol. 5, no. 3, sec. A.

need for us to debate the ends of our lives together in the university or college. Lacking any worthy end, we will be stuck with petty debates over administrative means and a university that only mirrors our surrounding cultural status quo rather than giving students the power to rise above it.

During our student years, we remember our restiveness under (what appeared to us) heavy-handed college administrators who were always telling students what to do. Thus our surprise to hear a sophomore say to us: "There's nobody at the top to say, 'Hey people, this is what this place is all about.'" A campus student activist noted, "We've got no philosophy of what the hell it is we want by the time somebody graduates. The so-called curriculum is a set of hoops that somebody says students ought to jump through before graduation. Nobody seems to have asked, 'How do people become good people?' We need more leadership from faculty and administration."

Lacking firm conviction about the type of students we want, unable ever to say to someone, "You have, by your actions, violated the spirit of life here and thereby forfeited your privilege to be here," we leave ourselves vulnerable to inappropriate intervention by those representing concerns other than the educational mission of the university.

A student administrator charged that "Lacking a coherent vision of why we are here, administration becomes the mere lunging into one crisis after another without anyone stepping back and asking, 'Why are we here?'" Two decades of allegedly value-neutral education have taken a heavy toll on the academy.

To some extent, every college and university — large or small — does have a philosophy of education. In most cases it has never been formalized and written down on a sheet of paper for circulation among faculty and students. Instead it exists only in the minds of the president and a handful of senior faculty.

There are several reasons why it may be beneficial for college faculty and administrators to develop a formal statement of educational philosophy. Often when administrators and faculty attempt to reach a consensus over the university's philosophy, they discover that different faculty members have radically different understandings of the school's fundamental principles. When there is no written statement spelling out the administration's basic principles, honest differences of opinion may go unnoticed for a long time; and they might be difficult to resolve when they do come to light. Perhaps that is one reason why we are fearful of a true debate over the means and the ends of our institutions of higher education. Lacking any statement of who we are, we are fearful that the debate would merely reveal our deep divisions and throw the entire institution into centrifuge.

Furthermore, the limitations of unwritten communications become more obvious the older the college or university becomes. Later-generation faculty and students who have never met the founders may have only a distorted view of the founders' original vision of the institution. An institution's purpose changes in subtle, unstated ways. Change is often necessary for an institution to survive in a changed world, but that change ought to be intentional and openly discussed. The older a college becomes and the more removed it is from the founders, the more important it is to have a written version of the college's educational philosophy.

The absence of an explicit, functioning educational philosophy implies a certain lack of discipline on the part of the faculty and senior administration, a lack of commitment to a specific set of principles. This lack of commitment soon becomes obvious to new faculty members, students, and nonacademic employees. Such an institution is easily manipulated by competitors, students, alumni, and — in the case of state universities — politicians. Sometime ago A. Bartlett Giamatti, former president of Yale, warned that many institutions of higher education display a "smugness that believes that the institution's value is so self-evident that it no longer needs explication, its mission so manifest that it no longer requires definition and articulation."[7]

A meaningful philosophy of education should address the questions: What does the educational process do *for* students, faculty, and those living in the larger community of which the university is

---

7. A. Bartlett Giamatti, *A Free and Ordered Space: The Real World of the University* (New York: Norton, 1988), p. 25.

a part? What does it do *to* students, faculty, and those in the surrounding environment? How do students and faculty *participate* in the educational process? An educational philosophy includes: (1) some notion of the meaning or purpose of education, (2) a statement of educational values, (3) ethical principles, and (4) a statement of social responsibility.

Surely the most difficult step for academic administrators in formulating an educational philosophy involves verbalizing one's sense of the *purpose* or *meaning* of higher education. Among the alternative purposes of higher education are:

1. To teach students how to *think* critically.
2. To facilitate students' *search for meaning.*[8]
3. To prepare students to live in a *democratic society.*
4. To train students for a specific *vocation.*
5. To raise the level of *self-confidence* of students.
6. To teach students how to *be.*[9]

Middlebury College's Purpose

Middlebury College's central purpose is to develop the life of the mind to the fullest sense: to foster clear and critical

---

8. For a full discussion of what we mean by "the search for meaning," see our book that arose out of our course at Duke University. Thomas H. Naylor, William H. Willimon, and Magdalena R. Naylor, *The Search for Meaning* (Nashville: Abingdon, 1994).

9. Edward LeRoy Long, Jr., lists the following "functional definition of educational purpose" as the responsibilities of an institution of higher education to its students:

1. the responsibility of the college or university for the identification, maturation, and enrichment of selfhood;
2. the responsibility of the college or university for the discovery/construction, extension, and dissemination of knowledge and culture;
3. the responsibility of the college or university for the well-being of society.

thinking, to disseminate valuable information, to facilitate research and to enrich the imagination, broaden sympathy and deepen insight. Middlebury seeks to help each student develop the capacity to contribute to society and find personal fulfillment.

Once trustees, administrators, and faculty have defined the purpose of higher education, they can then turn their attention to the difficult task of defining educational *values*. Values are social principles or standards by which we judge ourselves, which form a picture of who we want to be, aspects of the character we hope to have. Egalitarianism, individualism, communitarianism, self-improvement, and diversity are examples of educational values.

When 125 midshipmen (15 percent of the 1994 graduating class) were implicated in a cheating scandal at the United States Naval Academy, one could only wonder about the commitment to the Naval Academy's highly touted honor code by its students and administration. At least the Naval Academy was willing to discuss, and eventually even to discipline, those who had violated the code. How many other institutions of higher education would have the moral resources to do the same? One of the reasons why academic administrators have so much trouble dealing with such issues as "cultural diversity" and "political correctness" stems from a lack of well-defined academic values.

Ethics is a picture of what constitutes moral or immoral human conduct, an image of what sort of character we have. What constitutes ethical or unethical behavior depends on our sense of meaning, our habits, our virtues, and our values.

Some colleges and universities have attempted to operationalize their ethical principles and communicate them to students, faculty, and employees. These codes of ethics vary in length from one-page summaries of several ethical principles to lengthy, detailed treatments of educational policies covering many different aspects of academic life.

Given a set of values and ethical principles, how does one go about applying them to the various stakeholders of the university — administrators, faculty, students, nonacademic employees, alumni, financial contributors, and the general public? That is precisely the aim of a *statement of social responsibility*. Such a statement attempts to sort out the relative priority the administration assigns to each of the university's stakeholders.

Higher education dares not become merely the avenue to success; it must be the gateway for responsibility. It should not be concerned with competence alone, but with commitment to civic responsibility. An academic degree should not be a hunting license only for self-advancement, but an indication of abilities to seek, cultivate, and sustain a richer common weal. It is not enough to achieve cultural literacy; we must engender social concern. It is not enough merely to open the mind; it is necessary to cultivate moral intentionality in a total selfhood.[10]

Among the criticisms of today's graduates, we have heard not only the public's perception that they are often deficient in basic skills of effective communication and thought but also that these students are not prepared to contribute their part to the upbuilding and improvement of our society. They are individuals concerned exclusively with the attainment of individual goals. Even our very best graduates show a self-centeredness that renders them incapable of working in concert with others. The best know how to compete but not how to collaborate. In short, they have few skills for or little inclination toward social responsibility.

But then, consider who has been teaching these students. Each

10. Edward LeRoy Long, Jr., *Higher Education as a Moral Enterprise* (Washington, D.C.: Georgetown University Press, 1992), p. 221.

year, when the university awards PhDs, the president praises them for their "original, independent research." Original and independent may be another way of saying that these new scholars are prepared for a lifetime of independent, noncollaborative, lonely work. Faculty think of themselves as academic free agents, without much responsibility to the institution in which they serve, members of competing departments. No wonder that our students, particularly our best students who are most adept at fulfilling faculty expectations, may have the least sense of social responsibility.[11]

All too many statements of social responsibility turn out to be bland statements about apple pie, motherhood, and the flag. If a statement of social responsibility is to have any real bite, it must take a position on the relative importance of faculty, students, alumni, maintenance personnel — everyone concerned with the institution.

What good does a mere statement of purpose do? That depends upon how that statement is administered, how accountable we are held to it. At Duke, a supervisor of janitorial services told us that a cleaning person in one of the dorms was criticized by her immediate superior because she spent too much time talking to students in the dorms. She was accused of "playing Mama when she ought to be working as the maid." Yet the supervisor praised her for her work, saying, "All of us who work here are in the education business. That is the main goal. If a maid can be an educator of the young while she cleans the halls, then she is an example to the rest of us." We agree.

The entire credibility of the educational mission will be undermined if the mission statement says one thing but administrative behavior is antithetical to the stated philosophy. The philosophy should not make gratuitous statements about the importance of teaching, research, and service unless the administration is prepared to act accordingly.

With the lack of purpose and direction coming from the ad-

11. More than 80 percent of first-year college students said "developing a meaningful philosophy of life" was their prime college goal in the late 1960s, compared with 40 percent who said "being very well off financially" was their goal. By the late 1980s, the figures had reversed. Seventy-five percent now opted for financial security. Loeb, p. 13.

ministrative halls of many colleges and universities, it is hardly surprising to find college students struggling with such questions as:

1. Who am I?
2. Where am I going?
3. How can I prevent my life from being a series of accidents?
4. What do I want to be when I grow up?
5. How shall I overcome my separation from others, myself, and the ground of my being?
6. What alternatives are there to owning, possessing, manipulating, and controlling material goods, wealth, other people, and organizations?
7. Is it possible to experience meaning through *being* — through my creations, my personal relationships, the communities to which I belong, and my experience with pain, suffering, and eventually death.
8. Can I find meaningful employment?
9. Is it possible to experience real community?
10. How can I die happy?[12]

Plato's characterization of the youth of his time is a good depiction of the plight of American college students:

> [The democratic youth] lives along day by day, gratifying the desire that occurs to him, at one time drinking and listening to the flute, at another downing water and reducing, now practicing gymnastic, and again idling and neglecting everything; and sometimes spending his time as though he were occupied with philosophy. Often he engages in politics and, jumping up, says and does whatever chances to come to him; and if he admires any soldiers, he turns in that direction; and if it's moneymakers, in that one, and there is neither order nor necessity in his life, but calling it sweet, free and blessed, he follows it throughout.[13]

12. Naylor, Willimon, and Naylor, p. 113.
13. Plato, *Republic* 561c-d, cited in Allan Bloom, *The Closing of the American Mind* (New York: Simon and Schuster, 1987), pp. 87-88.

We do not know the social factors that contributed to youthful dislocation in Plato's time, but we do know that the factors contributing to the meaninglessness of the lives of college students today include inadequate parenting, the breakdown of the family, the absence of community, the ineffectiveness of public schools, and the declining influence of organized religion. Of course, these factors affect young adults whether or not they are on a college campus. Yet when we gather young adults in an expensive, privileged setting like today's campus, surely we ought carefully to consider the ways in which we can best assist them in the process of maturation and responsible development.

Bloom on Moral Education

The moral education that is today supposed to be the great responsibility of the family cannot exist if it cannot present to the imagination of the young a vision of a moral cosmos and of the rewards and punishments for good and evil, sublime speeches that accompany and interpret deeds, protagonists and antagonists in the drama of moral choice, a sense of the stakes involved in such choice, and the despair that results when the world is "disenchanted." Otherwise, education becomes the vain attempt to give children "values." Beyond the fact that parents do not know what they believe, and surely do not have the self-confidence to tell their children much more than that they want them to be happy and fulfill whatever potential they may have, values are such pallid things. What are they and how are they communicated? The courses in "value-clarification" springing up in schools are supposed to provide models for parents and get children talking about abortion, sexism or the arms race, issues the significance of which they cannot possibly understand. Such education is little more than propaganda . . . that does not work, because the opinions or values arrived at are will-o'-the-wisps, insubstantial, without ground in experience or passion, which are the bases of moral reasoning.[14]

In the 1960s, about 7 percent of college students came from homes where their parents were divorced. By the early 1990s, that number had risen to over 30 percent. College students who have experienced the pain of divorce and the absence of a parent, who have never known a real sense of community in their neighborhood or subdivision, who were bused across town to a public school connected to nothing, who are addicted to television and video games, and who have received no religious education whatsoever have their work cut out for themselves when they arrive on college campuses also steeped in meaninglessness. Back in the late 1960s, colleges and universities abandoned the *in loco parentis* approach to student life.[15] Unfortunately, we substituted little in its place. We abandoned the very generation of students who, having been inadequately parented and haphazardly educated, may have been least able to function left to themselves.

Bloom on Parenting

Parents do not have the legal or moral authority they had in the Old World. They lack self-confidence as educators of their children, generously believing that they will be better than their parents, not only in well-being, but in moral, bodily and intellectual virtue. There is always a

14. Bloom, pp. 60-61.
15. See Hoekema's excellent, succinct discussion of the rise and fall of *in loco parentis* as a legal principle in the first chapters of his *Campus Rules and Moral Community*.

more or less open belief in progress, which means the past appears poor and contemptible. The future, which is open-ended, cannot be prescribed to by parents, and it eclipses the past which they know to be inferior.

Along with the constant newness of everything and the ceaseless moving from place to place, first radio, then television, have assaulted and overturned the privacy of the home, the real American privacy, which permitted the development of a higher and more independent life within democratic society. Parents can no longer control the atmosphere of the home and have even lost the will to do so. With great subtlety and energy, television enters not only the room, but also the tastes of old and young alike, appealing to the immediately pleasant and subverting whatever does not conform to it. Nietzsche said the newspaper had replaced the prayer in the life of the modern bourgeois, meaning that the busy, the cheap, the ephemeral, had usurped all that remained of the eternal in his daily life. Now television has replaced the newspaper. It is not so much the low quality of the fare provided that is troubling. It is much more the difficulty of imagining any order of taste, any way of life with pleasures and learning that naturally fit the lives of the family's members, keeping itself distinct from the popular culture and resisting the visions of what is admirable and interesting with which they are bombarded from within the household itself.[16]

One of us well remembers, during the first days of college, a college assembly during which our president told the assembled freshmen, "You are among the best students ever to matriculate at Wofford College. You have the best high school records of any class before you. We are proud to have you as our students."

16. Bloom, pp. 58-59.

Then the president said something to us that is almost impossible to conceive of hearing today:

> Yet because most of you come from South Carolina, that means
> that most of you happen also to be racist. Your racial attitudes are
> mostly a matter of your history, your culture, the notions handed
> down to you by your parents. This college hopes to change that
> about you through your studies here. We hope to make you into
> the sort of people who will be able to know, from your education
> here, the error of such opinions as racial superiority. It will take
> us about four years to do this. And though we may not succeed
> in changing all of you, we hope to change enough of you to make
> a difference in our state in the future.

It is difficult to imagine a similar speech given by a college president today.

Recently it was revealed that more college women are having unsafe sex with partners. The more sexual experience college women acquire, the less likely they make sure their sexual partners use condoms, according to a survey by the University of Michigan, Ann Arbor. Of the college women surveyed, 76 percent were sexually active, averaging four partners. A mere 64 percent used protection during their first sexually active relationship; the number fell to 49 percent by the time they had sex with their fifth partner. Commenting on the results, Lisa Kaeser of the Alan Guttmacher Institute, New York, said the study shows "a frightening lack of knowledge of STDs among college women."[17] We suspect that "lack of knowledge" is not the problem. Something else is lacking.

We have come a long way, in American higher education, from there to here.

17. Marilyn Elias, "More Partners, More-Risky Sex," *USA Today*, November 12, 1994.

CHAPTER 5

All Things to All People

There seems only one cause behind all forms of social misery: Bigness. Oversimplified as this may seem, we shall find the idea more easily acceptable if we consider that bigness, or oversize, is really much more than just a social problem. It appears to be the one and only problem permeating all creation. Wherever something is wrong, something is too big.[1]

To undergraduates universities are landlords, to scholars they are multidisciplinary research institutes, to entrepreneurs they are science parks, to state government officials they are engines of economic growth, and to gung-ho alumni they are the sponsors of professional football and basketball teams disguised as college kids having a great time.[2] Is it any wonder that the cost of higher education is out of control and that the mission of most universities appears to be garbled and inconsistent? American universities have tried unsuccessfully to be everything to everybody. During higher education's "roaring eighties" we said no to almost no one. By the

1. Leopold Kohr, *The Breakdown of Nations* (New York: Dutton, 1978), p. xviii.
2. "Towers of Babble," *Economist*, December 25, 1993–January 7, 1994, p. 73.

nineties, we had become virtually unmanageable. This is a far cry from the fifties and sixties when universities were viewed by American conservatives as engines of economic growth, by liberals as agents of social change, and by taxpayers as avenues of social mobility.[3]

One of us followed Duke's past president into one of the dorms for an evening of dialogue with the students on any issue they wished to discuss. After an hour of discussion, the president left with this list of concerns:

1. The maid service in the dorms is lousy.
2. There were two broken toilet seats in the downstairs men's lavatory.
3. Can't something be done to get a janitor in the building on Sundays to clean up the mess that's left after the weekend parties?
4. Can Duke do something to arrange for live music on campus every Saturday night at a place where there is food and drink but where we can also dance?

Ah, the life of today's leader in higher education!

Even in the heyday of corporate mergers in the 1980s, few investors would have been attracted to conglomerates with portfolios as diverse and disjointed as those found in large universities today. American universities have become managerial behemoths. They are simply in too many unrelated, disconnected businesses.

Nothing better illustrates the compartmentalization that has occurred in colleges and universities than the separation that exists between undergraduate student life (food, housing, and social life) and undergraduate academic life. Student life and academic life will never be integrated unless the administration is seriously committed to making it happen. To whom does the dean of student life report? When the vice president for student life reports to the president, then student life is seen as another distinct area of administrative

3. "Towers of Babble," p. 73.

concern, like food services or athletics. The dean for student life should report to the senior undergraduate academic officer if student life is to be an integral part of campus academic life and not merely a social appendage.

Overspecialization and functional isolation are two of the reasons why college costs consistently outpace inflation. Each academic department or professional school is an island unto itself cooperating with no one. Promotions and faculty salaries are closely linked to publications within one's narrowly defined discipline. Departments compete with one another for students and resources. In this competitive environment new courses proliferate so as to attract more students and eventually more resources to a particular department.

Duke's business school, divinity school, engineering school, law school, and medical school each has its own separate library. The Fuqua School of Business at Duke also has its own hotel for executive education programs.

The cost of high-tech research equipment soared in the 1970s and 1980s — particularly in engineering, physical science, and medicine. The cost of research in such fields as particle physics and molecular biology is prohibitively expensive. But is all of this high technology and computer power really necessary to provide undergraduates with a well-rounded liberal arts education? We think not.

Undergraduate education and state-of-the-art research are two quite different businesses. Does it make any sense to try to combine them under one umbrella called a university? Middlebury College is an excellent undergraduate educational institution. MIT, Cal Tech, and the Stanford Research Institute are world-class research institutes. Should not Amherst, Middlebury, Mount Holyoke, Vassar, and Williams specialize in undergraduate teaching, and MIT, Cal Tech, and Carnegie-Mellon in basic and applied research? The necessary skills for successful research grantsmanship are not the same skills required to be a good undergraduate teacher. Why do so many academics pretend otherwise?

In all too many state universities and some private universities such as Duke, Notre Dame, and Southern California, intercollegiate athletics — particularly football and basketball — have achieved singular economic importance for the university. Big-time college foot-ball and basketball are high-profile businesses characterized by illegal recruiting, elaborate player perquisites, minimal academic standards, notoriously low graduation ratios, and a generally anti-intellectual ambiance. Even at private universities that presume to have higher academic standards for football and basketball players, athletes pursue an academic program of carefully monitored courses supported by an elaborate network of tutors and teaching assistants.

Throughout the 1980s, the University of North Carolina (UNC) lost many good faculty members because it could not afford to pay competitive academic salaries. But its alumni association had little difficulty in raising $33.8 million to finance its new indoor basketball stadium known as the "Dean Dome" — named after its highly successful basketball coach, Dean Smith. After a losing football season, UNC's booster club came up with an additional $1 million to buy out the football coach's contract ahead of schedule. Winning national football and basketball championships is far more important to most American universities than teaching young people how to think and find meaning in their lives.

As further evidence of the disproportionate amount of resources devoted to college football, consider the case of Mississippi — the poorest state in America. Although Ole Miss has only 8,500 under-graduates, its football stadium in Oxford will seat nearly 43,000 people. The stadiums at Mississippi State and Mississippi Southern seat 40,656 and 33,000, respectively. But these three universities play most of their home games in Jackson, whose stadium has a capacity of 60,492. Many colleges and universities, even during a winning season, fail to make profits from football. The expenditures are justified on the basis of morale or alumni support, even though there is some evidence that little correlation exists between a winning season and high alumni donations. Are these expenditures truly related to the goals of higher education?

College football and basketball are to the National Football League (NFL) and National Basketball Association (NBA) what the minor leagues are to professional baseball — training grounds for future major league athletes. The beauty of this corrupted system is that the member universities of the National Collegiate Athletic Association (NCAA) finance literally all of the preprofessional training for the pros who play in the NFL and the NBA, although only a tiny fraction of college players will ever become professional athletes.

Intercollegiate football and basketball are the academic equivalent of the Roman games. College sports heroes are treated like pagan Roman gladiators. They are strong, self-assertive, and narcissistic. We conveniently overlook the dirty mixture of money, greed, and publicity that surrounds big-time college football and basketball. Millions of American men and some women vicariously live out their fantasies of becoming college sports heroes by spending hours each week watching college football and basketball on television. Even more importantly, wealthy alumni and influential state legislators are entertained and made to feel good about their alma mater. This year the NCAA signed a $1.75-billion TV contract, to extend the next eight years, with CBS. But at what cost to the intellectual integrity of the institution?[4]

4. In 1903, Stanford's first president, David Starr Jordan, put it more bluntly (and honestly!) than we would dare today: "The athletic tramp should receive no academic welcome. The athletic parasite is no better than any other parasite. The man who is in college for athletics alone, disgraces the college, degrades athletics and shuts out a better man for his place on the team. In tolerating the presence of athletes who do not study, the college faculty becomes party to a fraud. Some of our greatest institutions stand disgraced in the eyes of the college world, by reason of the methods employed to win football victories." Quoted in David A. Hoekema, *Campus Rules and Moral Community: In Place of In Loco Parentis* (Lanham, Md.: Rowman & Littlefield Pub., 1994), p. 45.

"Male varsity athletes are more likely to be accused of sexual assault than are students who do not play varsity sports, according to a new study. The study, by researchers at Northeastern University and the University of Massachusetts at Amherst, was based on police records from 20 Division I colleges. . . . while male athletes accounted for 3.7 per cent of the male students at 20 of the participating colleges, they were named in 5.3 per cent of the sexual assaults." *Chronicle of Higher Education,* December 7, 1994, p. A37.

SIS BOOM DUH

College men have begun kicking the old pigskin around. But how are the nation's scholar-athletes doing off the field?[5]

School	Football Team Graduation Rate
Clemson	42%
Southern California	42%
Arizona	40%
Alabama	39%
Texas A & M	38%
Florida	37%
Washington	30%
Ohio State	29%

Although the NCAA does not permit college athletes to be paid to promote consumer products on television, college coaches are allowed to be free agents on this unregulated playing field. Students and alumni alike were chagrined to learn that Duke's charismatic basketball coach, Mike Krzyzewski, had reportedly signed a seven-figure "shoe contract" with Nike "to keep Duke University in Nikes." The buying of college coaches is a widespread practice among well-known consumer-goods manufacturers.

The Selling of the University

Nike Inc. . . . . has agreed to provide Michigan with about $1-million a year in shoes, uniforms, and scholarship money for seven years. In exchange, Michigan will allow

5. *Time*, September 12, 1994, p. 36.

the company to use the university's logo in its advertisements.[6]

We take great pride that Duke enjoys one of the highest football-team graduation rates in the country. But Duke is an exception. Coaches who fail to be educators should cease to be college coaches. In stark contrast to all of this unseemly intercollegiate athletic razzmatazz are the athletic programs at small colleges like Middlebury that give no athletic scholarships. Students are students first and athletes second. Four out of ten Middlebury students play varsity athletics, and students also take part in club, intramural, and individual sports. Middlebury women play eleven varsity sports and men play twelve. The college has extensive state-of-the-art athletic facilities as well as its own top-quality alpine and Nordic skiing areas located twelve miles from campus. For alpine skiing, the Snow Bowl has fourteen trails, three chair lifts, snowmaking equipment, and a ski lodge with a snack bar, reading room, and mountain views.

Duke has launched a multimillion-dollar drive to improve its extensive intramural facilities. Athletics, far from being the great destroyer of educational integrity, can be a major source of faculty-student interaction, a source of holistic intellectual engagement — if colleges and universities recover a strong sense of their primary educational mission and make their decisions about athletics on the basis of that sense of mission.

There are 3,400 private and public institutions of higher learning in America ranging from small liberal arts colleges, to two-year community colleges and technical institutions, to state colleges and universities, to flagship research universities. Although many small liberal arts colleges and some major private universities like Chicago, Duke, and Stanford have wisely kept a lid on growth, the prevailing attitude among most state universities, caught in the competition for

6. *Chronicle of Higher Education,* November 30, 1994, p. A41.

tax dollars since World War II, has been "growth for growth's sake" and "bigger makes better." The trend toward growth has decidedly slowed as we move through the nineties. Now we find ourselves burdened with huge institutions in serious need of downsizing.

We believe that there are far too many universities in the United States. Some are so tiny that it is difficult to take their self-proclaimed university status seriously. Others are so large that they are fundamentally unmanageable. The state of North Carolina, for example — a relatively poor state with a population of 6.8 million — has no fewer than fifteen state universities plus another seven private universities. The state also has four medical schools — two public and two private. When Western Carolina College was given university status by the North Carolina legislature a number of years ago, the college's president was asked by a radio announcer, "What changes do you anticipate now that Western Carolina has become a university?" He responded, "I really haven't thought much about it." Racial politics in Mississippi — a state with only 2.6 million people — has resulted in eight public universities in a state that can hardly afford to support one. On the other hand, tiny Vermont with a population of 570,000 sensibly has only one state university.

However, some Vermonters question whether their state has the resources to continue supporting a university that is all too dependent on the high tuition it charges out-of-state students. Among the questions that ought to be asked by Vermont politicians is, "Why does UVM have two business schools — one ostensibly to train executives for Fortune 500 companies, of which there are virtually none in Vermont, and the other to train managers of small agribusinesses?" Others ought to raise doubts about the state's ability to afford a fully integrated, high-tech medical school — particularly when Vermont is surrounded by four of the best medical schools in the country: Cornell, Dartmouth, Yale, and Harvard.

Bigness and Badness

There is no misery on earth that cannot be successfully handled on a small scale as, conversely, there is no misery on earth that can be handled at all *except* on a small scale. In vastness, everything crumbles, even the good, because the world's one and only problem is not wretchedness but bigness.[7]

The proliferation of universities with the inherent duplication of programs, research facilities, libraries, athletic programs, and academic infrastructure has contributed significantly to the skyrocketing cost of higher education. America needs not more universities but more small undergraduate colleges. Plato believed that the ideal republic would have no more than about 5,832 citizens, in order adequately to foster communication and argument. But we have acted as if sheer size makes no difference when it comes to achieving the mission of higher education. The students themselves seem instinctively to know that much is at stake in the issue of institutional size. After "academic reputation" and "graduates get good jobs," "size of college" was listed by the 1994 freshmen as the most important factor in selecting a college.[8]

Just as there are too many small universities whose quest for university status has distracted them from the tasks of undergraduate education, there are also too many universities that have become inefficient, dehumanized, bureaucratic agglomerations of unrelated businesses. Undergraduate, professional, graduate, and adult education; housing; food service; dental and health care services; book publishing; agricultural extension service; management consulting; public service; and semiprofessional athletics are among the plethora of unrelated businesses in which large universities find themselves.

7. Kohr, p. 79.
8. "This Year's Freshmen: A Statistical Profile," *Chronicle of Higher Education,* January 13, 1995, p. A31.

With 52,183 students, 38,958 of whom are undergraduates, the Columbus campus of Ohio State University is the largest university in the United States. Arizona State, Michigan State, Ohio State, Penn State, Texas A & M, and the Universities of Michigan, Minnesota, Texas, and Wisconsin are more like small cities than academic communities.

Mega-Universities[9]

Enrollment

Arizona State University	43,635
Indiana University	36,076
Michigan State University	40,047
Ohio State University	52,183
Pennsylvania State University	38,446
Texas A & M	41,710
University of Michigan	36,626
University of Minnesota	38,019
University of Texas	49,253
University of Wisconsin	43,196

Most of these universities are the legacy of World War II and postwar growth rather than serious academic planning. Is quality undergraduate education compatible with so diverse a portfolio of unrelated activities? We believe that it is time for us to take a critical look at the businesses of these mega-universities. Do mega-universities represent a cost-effective way to train future generations of Americans? Has the time come to begin seriously thinking about downsizing these academic giants?

Throughout the 1960s many universities grew haphazardly

9. From *Petersons' Guide to Four Year Colleges,* 24th ed. (Princeton: Petersons' Guides, 1994).

without any well-defined sense of direction. It is as though some of them have attempted to replicate urban sprawl in an academic setting. New programs are generated by a combination of the latest academic fads and new sources of government funding. Not unlike the programs of the federal government, obsolete academic programs are seldom allowed to die. Instead, they continue indefinitely long after the original program rationale has faded.

Although strategic planning became a popular buzzword in higher education in the 1980s, at many institutions of higher education it was a mere public relations gimmick aimed at private foundations and government agencies. Top-down strategic planning without serious faculty, student, and employee input is merely an irrelevant academic exercise. No one is committed to anything. Tough choices are avoided. Those who are expected to implement the strategies required to achieve the institution's goals and objectives should participate actively in the formulation of the university's goals, objectives, and strategies. Furthermore, university-wide strategies cut across departmental, professional school, and program boundaries and necessarily require interdisciplinary teams if they are to be viable. Large universities are too complex to be managed by a handful of isolated administrators sitting in an ivory tower.

We therefore agree with the Pew Roundtable's call for colleges and universities to "Engage faculty as primary agents in the process of reform, to simplify the curriculum in ways that ensure that full-time faculty teach core courses, to become smaller, more efficient institutions less committed to employment for its own sake, and to establish principles making each unit accountable for balancing its own budget. . . . Higher education remains an enterprise too often prone to define progress in terms of addition rather than substitution or subtraction."[10]

Would we be willing to submit our students to the evaluation of the larger community, letting our constituents in business, industry, the professions, and the arts evaluate how well we are doing,

10. "Policy Perspectives," *Pew Higher Education Roundtable,* April 1994, vol. 5, no. 3, sec. A.

based upon their assessment of our students? That is exactly what Alverno College in Milwaukee does. Alverno recruited and trained a team of community advisers to help the college guide and evaluate its students in what it calls "Outcome Based Education." Four European countries — Britain, Denmark, France, and the Netherlands — now have national systems in place to evaluate and rank the overall quality of their institutions of higher education.[11] Most of us would be nervous to submit the "products" of our education to the critical gaze of the larger community. And yet, if the larger community loses faith in our ability to educate, it may take its resources elsewhere.[12]

The Mission of Duke University

The founding Indenture of Duke University directed the members of the university to "develop our resources, increase our wisdom, and promote human happiness."

To these ends, the mission of Duke University is to provide a superior liberal education to undergraduate students, attending not only to their intellectual growth but also to their development as adults committed to high ethical standards and full participation as leaders in their communities; to prepare future members of the learned professions for lives of skilled and ethical service by providing excellent graduate and professional education; to

11. *Chronicle of Higher Education,* December 7, 1994, p. A41.

12. Duke's president, Nannerl O. Keohane, in speaking of higher education's responsibility to its benefactors, says, "We are held by the public, . . . to a different standard from the for-profit world, and this is as it should be. We must carefully consider our stewardship of the financial resources entrusted to our care and give an open and accurate accounting of how those resources have been used. . . . we must be particularly careful about the salaries we pay our senior executives. . . . If a handsome income is your goal in life, you should be in some other line of work." We applaud President Keohane's awareness of our accountability to our benefactors. *Chronicle of Higher Education,* December 7, 1994, p. B5.

advance the frontiers of knowledge and contribute boldly to the international community of scholarship; to foster health and well-being through medical research and patient care; and to promote a sincere spirit of tolerance, a sense of the obligations and rewards of citizenship, and a commitment to learning, freedom and truth.

By pursuing these objectives with vision and integrity, Duke University seeks to engage the mind, elevate the spirit, and stimulate the best effort of all who are associated with the university; to contribute in diverse ways to the local community, the state, the nation and the world; and to attain and maintain a place of real leadership in all that we do.

All of the means to duplicate the work of higher education are already in place in other institutions. The world may discover that there are more efficient places to learn a foreign language than a four-year college. Technology promises to make instruction accessible to people in the privacy of their homes. While universities still enjoy an exclusive hold on the credentialing and accrediting process for teachers, doctors, and lawyers, that may not always be the case. These privileges can be withdrawn if the professions feel that university-based training is not cost-effective for the goals of their professions. We predict that more people will be asking in the future, "What do colleges and universities do that no other institution can do?"

Declining college enrollment application pools suggest that the process of downsizing has already begun.

We believe that the path forward begins with a look backward, back to the basic unit of education, namely, the teacher engaged with a student. That is the source from which education's power flows, the holy moment at the heart of the enterprise. Developmentally speaking, the abandonment of the young to their own devices, aggregating them in huge conclaves of postadolescent isolation, is a strange, developmentally inappropriate way to lead the young into adulthood. The largest university and the smallest liberal arts college exist mainly for fostering the sacred exchange between teacher and student. We must evaluate all programs by how well they contribute to this educational interaction. We must remind ourselves that this is the reason we are here.

Hey, this is a university for God's sake! This isn't a damn bar. These guys don't know nothing about running bars. All they're good at is teaching people. If you want a drink, go to somebody who knows something about it for God's sake. You go to a university to learn.

*A student comment after a two-hour
meeting on alcohol policy in the university*

CHAPTER 6

Where Is the Glue?

It is enacted, that scholars of all conditions shall keep away from inns, eating-houses, wine-shops, and all houses whatever within the city, or precinct of the University, wherein wine or any other drink, or the Nicotean herb, or tobacco, is commonly sold; also that if any person does otherwise, and is not eighteen years old, and not a graduate, he shall be flogged in public.[1]

The day has past when college administrators had either the authority or the inclination of Archbishop Laud to flog young scholars for their misbehavior. *In loco parentis* (in place of parents) has gone the way of the freshman beanie, not to be replaced by *in loco avunculi* (in place of uncles) or even *in loco avi* (in place of grandparents). Modern colleges and universities therefore search for an answer to the question, What responsibility do we owe our students and what responsibility do they owe us? Where is the glue that holds us together on campus?

When Harvard's Arthur Levine asked students on the eve of their graduation in 1980 which image stood out in their minds as

1. William Laud, archbishop of Canterbury and chancellor of Oxford University, *Laud's Code,* 1636. Quoted by David A. Hoekema, *Campus Rules and Moral Community: In Place of In Loco Parentis* (Lanham, Md.: Rowman & Littlefield Pub., 1994), p. vii.

capturing the spirit of their age, they said Vietnam and Watergate. These events defined them, formed their outlook. When Levine repeated his survey in 1993, the predominant image mentioned was the *Challenger* explosion. As one student described that event to one of us, "It was a sign that everything was blowing apart."[2]

What does it mean to be educating a generation whose central image of their world is an elementary-school teacher being blown up in a spacecraft?

Our institutions of higher education are in centrifuge. They are coming unglued. Not only have we allowed the size of universities to reach dehumanized proportions, but we have structured the modern university in such a way that the chances of faculty befriending students are slim. Detachment is the ruling mode. Forgetting the etymology of the term *professor* as "someone who professes something," we are more inclined as faculty to say "the data show . . ." rather than "I have found . . ." or "I believe that. . . ." Classes and curricula are structured so that faculty and students will be as much strangers to one another when they leave the university as when they arrived.

We say we are disengaged from our students' lives because we "trust them," we "give them responsibility," or we "allow them to be adults." This is rather thin rationalization for our abandonment of them. We use the students to finance our writing and research, as a base from which to promote ourselves within our professional guilds and disciplines, but we do not really engage them in education.

In an extended conversation with Women's Studies faculty, one of us was told that the primary reason twelve women students transferred from the university the previous year was the "anti-intellectual" climate at the university. (From our own observations, far more women than men criticize this aspect of the school.) The Women's Studies professors believe there is too little appreciation for the holistic learning that occurs outside the classroom. And, while the students receive an education outside the classroom, it may not be one we want to support.

2. See Arthur Levine, *When Dreams and Heroes Died* (San Francisco: Jossey-Bass, 1980).

"What could we do better to process in the classroom the events from outside of the classroom?" these faculty asked. "The students crave to have more of us." Others seem to agree. A 1989 study of seven areas of educational practice by the Carnegie Council on Policy Studies in Higher Education was most emphatic on one point: undergraduate education in America could be improved if more attention were given to the emotional and social development of students.[3]

Some of us faculty have been guilty of what Sharon Parks has called "overdistancing."[4] While it is appropriate to allow young adults to experiment with different modes of living, to try out ideas and insights free of adult domination, we have moved from a developmentally healthy distancing to a developmentally detrimental virtual abandonment.

The Student as Consumer

[T]he creation of community in the educational process has been made problematic by the shift of paradigm from one that portrays the relationship between student and teacher as that between apprentice and mentor to one more analogous to the relationship between a consumer and a provider of services.[5]

Those who work with students frequently recall the bygone days of the *in loco parentis* policies, the alleged modus operandi of colleges and universities until at least the early 1960s. Up until that time, most college and university administrators (and there were an

3. As reported in *The Chronicle of Higher Education*, April 14, 1989.
4. Sharon Parks, *The Critical Years: The Young Adult Search for a Faith to Live By* (San Francisco: Harper & Row, 1986), p. 172.
5. Edward LeRoy Long, Jr., *Higher Education as a Moral Enterprise* (Washington, D.C.: Georgetown University Press, 1992), p. 52.

amazingly small number of administrators on campus until the sixties) took an unashamedly parental approach to students. Of course, except for the postwar years, most students were fresh out of high school. Then, beginning in the sixties, the *in loco parentis* ideology was replaced by a new ideology, demanded by the students, of individual autonomy (literally "self law"), freedom, and a minimum amount of administrative intervention into their lives.

We recall a conversation one of us had with the Student Affairs Committee in a meeting some cynically referred to as "damage control," the mopping-up action after a weekend of student carousing and vandalizing. A newcomer to the scene, I blurted out, "Can't something be done about this? Don't you think it is a shame that these people come to us with such potential and then waste themselves with alcohol?"

A dean responded, "But what can we do? After all, we are not their parents."

"We are not their parents," agreed the questioner, "but could we at least be their older brothers and sisters? Could we be their friends?"

Might the modern university consider playing the role, not of substitute parent, but of wise friend?

"It is important that we give students their freedom," many respond. "Freedom is developmentally important. We need to treat students like adults, relying on them to make mature decisions for themselves."

But the majority of undergraduate students are not adults. At best a student is, in Daniel Levinson's words, "a novice adult."[6] Younger students are not capable of "making their own decisions" or "thinking for themselves." Leaving them to themselves, with no skills for discernment, with their meager personal experience and a narrow worldview, they become the willing victims of the most totalitarian form of government ever devised — namely, submission to their peers, obeisance to people just like them. This is not freedom.

How do people grow up and develop social skills and critical

6. Daniel Levinson, *The Seasons of a Man's Life* (New York: Ballantine Books, 1979), pp. 73-111.

thinking ability? Not through exercising some abstract "freedom" but rather by observing, imitating, confronting, and arguing with those with more experience in life. So Neil Postman, in *Technopoly: The Surrender of Culture to Technology*,[7] urges all teachers, no matter what their subject, to regard themselves as historians: those who initiate the young into adulthood by sharing with them what humanity has learned thus far. Unfortunately, faculty and adults are mostly absent from campus, especially during evening hours and weekends, when students are most socially active. Even during lunch hours, faculty eat in their offices or in restricted faculty dining rooms. Thus opportunities for students to observe their elders are severely limited.

Could it not be argued that there is an interesting relationship between good teaching and good parenting? Rejecting *in loco parentis* has rendered the university a sterilized community without the "diversity" we say we crave. Diversity, the ability to be different, to enjoy one's differences, to stand alone against the crowd if needed, to exercise bold thought and judgment, to confront the richness of human differences in others, may be in great part fostered by the values that our elders demonstrate in their lives and teaching. Alexis de Tocqueville noted that Americans created a culture in which everyone was free to say whatever he wanted — yet unfortunately everyone chose to say the same thing. Freedom and individuality are complex. What conditions help create free people?

A person who has spent many years counseling students on our campus noted that a better empirical case could be made for supporting *in loco parentis* during the nineties than during the fifties. Increasing numbers of our students have been inadequately parented. They arrive on campus having missed important aspects of human development — interaction and conflict with their parents over values. They were left to their own devices. These are not people yearning to be left alone by adults. In our first-year seminar, "The Search for Meaning,"[8] we ask students to write a short "personal

---

7. Neil Postman, *Technopoly: The Surrender of Culture to Technology* (New York: Knopf, 1992).
8. See our reference to our book, *The Search for Meaning*, in chapter 4.

history paper." This past year, seven of the sixteen students who submitted papers mentioned that the most determinative, life-changing event for them was their parents' divorce. Only one mentioned a father. It was as if these young people were orphans.

One of the explanations for the current state of the university is that universities are being run by people who were themselves students in the sixties, when their supreme value was an abstract notion of freedom. These were the students who fought for, and achieved, the abolition of rules and structures, and who removed faculty and administrative interference in student life. Their main educational agenda could be characterized as "breaking away." Education is what you do when you flee some restrictive, small-town environment for the liberating freedom of college. Now that they are in positions of power, these products of the sixties run the university much as they wanted it administered when they were students.

Unfortunately, many of these "tenured radicals"[9] fail to realize that we are dealing with a very different generation of students, students whose developmental and educational agenda is quite different from the one we had when we were students. Today's students do not seem obsessed by the search for freedom, the need for "breaking away." They seem much more interested in the search for roots, stability, order, and identity. A number of college administrators, who remember the rebellious students of the 1960s, expressed their amazement that today's students are eager to embrace school traditions and ceremonies, seeing this eagerness as some means of gaining a past among a generation without memory. Many of today's students are convinced that modern life is chaotic, essentially unmanageable, impenetrable by human action. Perhaps one of the causes of their passivity is that they have no memory, no real awareness of history, so they have lost hope that anything they decide or do can possibly impact the shape of the world.[10]

9. See the somewhat overdrawn blame of the sixties for our present crisis in Roger Kimball, *Tenured Radicals: How Politics Has Corrupted Our Higher Education* (New York: HarperCollins, 1990).

10. Paul Rogat Loeb quotes Christopher Lasch in his observation that our young have no hope for the future, in great part, because we have left them ignorant

The university's lack of coherence may be one factor behind the explosion of administrative budgets in the 1980s. Expenditures for deans, presidents, and all their assistants grew 26 percent faster than instructional budgets. Salaries for administrators and other nonteaching personnel are now almost half of the amount of college budgets spent on actual teaching.[11]

Have we attempted to solve our problem of campus fragmentation by hiring more bureaucrats who write and administer more rules? Bureaucrats and rules do not a college make.

Campus Rules

Many of the problems of student conduct — excessive drinking, cheating, sexual exploitation — have existed for generations and will doubtless plague future generations of administrators in their turn. But the task of countering improper behavior has become more complex, as student rights to privacy and autonomy have come to be more generally recognized at the same time that the responsibility for setting and enforcing policies has become concentrated more and more in the hands of administrators. The help of the faculty in both setting and enforcing conduct standards has never been more urgently needed — and it has perhaps never been less frequently offered.[12]

---

of their past: "If young people feel no connection to anything, their dislocation is a measure of our failure, not theirs. We have failed to provide them with a culture that claims to explain the world or that links the experience of one generation to those that came before and to those that will follow." Quoted by Loeb, *A Generation at the Crossroads: Apathy and Action on the American Campus* (New Brunswick, N.J.: Rutgers University Press, 1994), p. 126.

11. Barbara R. Bergmann, "Bloated Administration, Blighted Campuses," *Academe,* November-December 1991, pp. 12-16.

12. Hoekema, p. 61.

We cannot reinstitute *in loco parentis*. Yet might it be possible for the university to act *in loco amicis,* as a wise friend? Loneliness appears to be built into our present system. What can we do at the modern university to nurture friendship between adults and those who are becoming adults and to explore friendship as the normative means of education? Aristotle noted that friendship "holds states together" (*Nicomachean Ethics*). Today's university (a misnamed institution if ever there were one) is neither unified nor coherent. Years ago Clark Kerr tried to put a positive face upon our fragmentation by renaming us the "multiversity." In many cases our much-praised "diversity" is but the latest attempt to speak positively of the fact that we have nothing to hold us together. We desperately need a glue to join the parts into a whole — some relatively commonly affirmed goals and means. Although Aristotle was skeptical that true friendship could occur among the young — because "their lives are guided by emotion, and they pursue most intensely what they find pleasant and what the moment brings," so that they "become friends quickly and just as quickly cease to be friends" — Aristotle did believe that friendship was one of the supreme intellectual virtues to be cultivated. The campus, as a place set apart, and the undergraduate years, as time set apart, should provide an ideal opportunity for friendship to flourish. "Time and familiarity are required" for Aristotelian friendship.[13]

Might it be possible for the university to become a place where people are allowed the time and the space for friendship to develop, where the virtues required of friends are cultivated, and where we all become more adept in the art of relating to one another not as strangers, adversaries, clients, customers, or care-givers, but as friends?[14] Might all of us recover a sense that the point of teaching is friendship rather than mere transference of knowledge? Again, Aristotle taught that friendship was the foundation of teaching.

13. *Aristotle: Nicomachean Ethics,* trans. Martin Ostwald (New York: Macmillan, 1962).
14. A good place to begin is to have faculty and students read together Eudora Welty and Ronald A. Sharp's collection in *The Norton Book of Friendship* (New York: Norton, 1991).

This can apply to the problem of alcohol abuse. "Friends don't let friends drive drunk," says the advertising slogan. The thought is not trite. What might it mean if we viewed alcohol use, for example, not as an issue of rules and regulations, solely an administrative responsibility, but as an issue related to education in the virtues of friendship? Might the university become a prophetic place where the status quo in our society is not merely mirrored but rather prophetically criticized? There is something terribly wrong where we allow talented people to destroy themselves in self-destructive behavior while we mouth platitudes about individual freedom and autonomy. Might the university put its talented minds to the task of envisioning new structures of caring and community?

A Duke student, concerned about the problems both of drunken driving after campus parties and the safety of women on campus at night, developed the "Safe Rides Program." Anyone, at any time of night, can call a number and receive a free, safe ride home with no questions asked.

At William and Mary, students run an alcohol-free coffee house with student entertainment in a fun setting. Texas Christian asked students to list students whom they would turn to with a problem. The most frequently identified individuals were asked to serve as mentors. They were trained to identify student problems and to respond to them in informed, caring, and intelligent ways. Johns Hopkins now includes substance-abuse identification and training as part of its orientation for new faculty.

Thus David A. Hoekema acknowledges that *in loco parentis* is dead, then searches for its replacement. He finds hope in the emergence and increasing prominence of various "communities" on campus, small groups — social, political, academic, religious — where students and faculty have the opportunity for quality interaction concerning things that matter. Hoekema says,

> these groups make an indispensable contribution to the formation of moral maturity in students. . . . moral conviction and moral action can be instilled only in the company of others. We learn to be moral by modeling ourselves on others whose judgment and

94

integrity we respect. Even when we reject or surpass our models, we do so in a social context. . . . to rely on ever more strenuous enforcement of disciplinary rules and codes is an inherently ill-suited tactic. . . . Institutions ought rather to devote their efforts to systematic encouragement of smaller communities contained on campus in which moral reflection and thoughtful choice flourish.[15]

We believe that friendship could be a guiding metaphor, the "glue" for our life together on today's campus. Some may think that our thoughts relate only to the "traditional" undergraduate, the youth fresh out of high school, those whom we have in high proportions at places like Middlebury and Duke. Yet friendship is an appropriate goal and a difficult attainment for students at any age. Faculty as well. In fact, faculty — most of whom have been trained, if trained at all, in very limited methods of classroom teaching, specialists in the art of working in lonely isolation — may be higher education's greatest challenge in rethinking itself. In a society that too often is a conglomeration of detached and isolated individuals, we call for a rediscovery of the idea of a college as a place where talented youth have the privileged time and the space set apart to become friends. Hannah Arendt noted that, missing the "political" implications of friendship, "we are wont to see friendship solely as a phenomenon of intimacy, in which the friends open their hearts to each other unmolested by the world and its demands." She challenges this view as a modern perversion, defending the Aristotelian idea that friendship is the basis of the polis, the first building block of the good society. Friendship is not merely some one-to-one intimacy. Friendship is the tough, long-term, often painful struggle to form community. Arendt recalls the relationship between friendship and conversation:

> For the Greeks the essence of friendship consisted in discourse. They held that only the constant interchange of

15. Hoekema, pp. 158-59.

talk united citizens in a *polis.* . . . The Greeks called this humanness which is achieved in the discourse of friendship *philanthropia,* "love of man," since it manifests itself in a readiness to share the world with other men. Its opposite, misanthropy, means simply that the misanthrope finds no one with whom he cares to share the world, that he regards nobody as worthy of rejoicing with him in the world and nature and the cosmos.[16]

We dream of colleges and universities where mature adults eagerly share with those on their way to maturity the discourse of friendship.

16. Hannah Arendt, *Men in Dark Times* (New York: Harcourt, Brace, 1968), pp. 24-25.

THE SOLUTION

CHAPTER 7

Restructuring Higher Education

In an aggressive effort to remedy ills common to many of the nation's small liberal arts colleges, Bennington College is reducing tuition, trimming its staff, and eliminating tenure.

The private, four-year college in Bennington, Vermont, said it embarked on the program to help close a $1 million deficit and to increase enrollment, which has fallen to 450 students from a high of 600 five years ago in part because of the high cost of attending the institution.

> "Had Bennington done nothing, the future of this institution was seriously in doubt," said the college president, Elizabeth Coleman. ". . . [F]iscal urgencies were present, but so were educational ones."
>
> The college has always been regarded as iconoclastic. . . . Now it is eliminating its academic departments; a core faculty of 45 to 50 professors, augmented by visiting specialists, will now teach across disciplines. . . .
>
> Speaking of Bennington's program, David Merkowitz, a spokesman for the American Council on Education, . . . said, "This kind of effort is . . . the kind of thing that a smaller, private institution can do more easily than a larger private institution or a public university."
>
> . . . Bennington's plan, like restructuring plans at other colleges,

99

drew criticism from the American Association of University Professors, which said it was "deeply concerned."[1]

Throughout the early 1990s, hardly a week went by without another major American company announcing layoffs of several thousand employees. The list of premier companies engaged in downsizing or restructuring includes AT&T, General Motors, Procter & Gamble, and Xerox, to mention only a few. There is an increasing realization that being bigger does not yield increased efficiency. The so-called "law of increasing returns to scale," which misled us into believing that average costs would decrease over time with increases in company size, turns out to be a myth. If output continues to grow for a firm, there is some point beyond which additional increments in production result in reduced efficiency and the firm may eventually become completely unmanageable. As the size of the firm increases, problems of motivation, coordination, communication, and control become more acute. Productivity decreases. The combined effect of increased global competition and decreasing returns to scale has forced hundreds of large American corporations to restructure themselves.

The dramatic changes that were shaking American business found no parallel on our college and university campuses. Most of our institutions of higher education proceeded along the same paths to which they had grown accustomed after World War II. Although blue-collar wages tripled, the average full professor's salary at private institutions quadrupled. Tuition at four-year private institutions is about seven times higher than it was twenty years ago. The rise in

1. "Radical Answer to a Small College's Woes," *New York Times,* June 23, 1994, p. A12. See Mark Edmundson, "Bennington Means Business," *New York Times Magazine,* October 23, 1994, pp. 42-76, for a full discussion of Bennington's recent restructuring. Also, "Innovation or Ruin?" *Chronicle of Higher Education,* November 30, 1994, p. A19. Internal critics have charged that Bennington has suffered more than a major restructuring. They charge that Bennington has abandoned its mission. If they are right, then the Bennington situation shows the great dangers of having restructuring forced upon us by financial exigencies rather than through careful, thoughtful, participatory planning. Many other schools must act now if they are to avoid the dilemma of Bennington.

costs at state-supported colleges has grown only slightly less rapidly. Columnist Robert Reno, in reporting these dramatic increases, notes that they occurred "Absent an explosion in the quality of higher education and in the competence of graduates during the same period. . . . it is pretty obvious that the finances of the nation's colleges and universities, were they viewed with the scrutiny we apply to most public expenditures or to ordinary household budgets, are out of control."[2] Some of the increased budgets of institutions of higher education can be attributed to government mandates, health care costs, increased security costs, and technology requirements rather than simple institutional greed. Yet the costs, whatever their source, are a major factor in the current crisis.

Academic Budgets

From 1982 to 1992, the proportion of the budgets that colleges spent on instruction fell from 32.4 percent to 30.7 percent. . . . Spending on libraries fell from 2.7 percent to 2.3 percent and on maintenance from 8.4 percent to 6.6 percent. On the other hand, administrative budgets increased 45 percent at private universities. . . . "It raises the question of what educational institutions are for," said James Perley, a biology professor at the College of Wooster in Ohio.[3]

We believe there are striking parallels to the problems of corporate America in most American universities. Although tuition con

2. Robert Reno, "Higher Education Costs Choking Middle Class," *Burlington Free Press,* August 31, 1994. See also "Price of Higher Education Becomes Even Dearer," *New York Times,* September 27, 1994.

3. Jon Marcus, "Tuitions Continue to Spiral," Associated Press, September 27, 1994.

tinues to spiral upwards, the quality and real economic value of undergraduate education are declining. Too many teachers teach too little, and students take too few courses. The prevailing values on college campuses are individualism, hedonism, and anti-intellectualism. When a Columbia University study proclaims that "binge drinking is the number one substance abuse problem in American college life,"[4] that finding is stark testimony to the nihilism that infects the academy.

All of this became painfully, personally obvious in the early 1980s, when Susanne Naylor, the daughter of one of us, entered Boston University as a first-year student. With over 25,000 students, the enrollment at BU exceeded the population of the town of Chapel Hill where Susanne had grown up. She was assigned a dormitory room in Warren Towers — a grotesque structure consisting of three eighteen-floor towers covering an entire city block. Susanne reported that weekends in the cinder-block halls of Warren Towers, thick with the aroma of marijuana and vomit, resembled life in a pigsty. Despite BU president John Silber's reputation as a no-nonsense disciplinarian, Susanne found the party atmosphere at BU to be depressingly anti-intellectual. Courses, often taught by graduate students, were lacking in content. Yet BU's tuition (and the president's salary) was among the highest in the nation.

College dormitories are too often just that — sleeping places, where the chaos that reigns on most nights makes any other kind of activity, like studying, conversation, and argument, impossible. Warehoused in high-rise dorms, treated as a number rather than a name, is it any wonder that at this vulnerable, unstable time in life, thousands of young adults are being put at increased risk just by the form that undergraduate life has taken at many large schools?

We believe that what is called for in higher education is nothing less than a complete restructuring of universities including the way they are organized, the way undergraduates are taught, and the substance of the curriculum. The ultimate aim of restructuring is to improve the quality of undergraduate education, increase its value,

4. As reported in the *New York Times,* June 11, 1994, p. B21.

102

and reduce its cost — to create a community of scholars and teachers that will enhance students' critical thinking skills and their search for meaning.

Why Did I Leave College Teaching?

Why did I leave college teaching? I was teaching a math class for freshmen. One morning I was calling the roll and noted that Jim was absent again.

"Where is Jim?" I asked. The class sat there with a stunned, horrified look on their faces.

"Haven't you heard?" one of them asked.

"Heard what?" I asked.

"Jim died last night. Well, actually, he killed himself, jumped out of his dorm window down to the quad."

I was devastated. Yet more devastation was to come. As Jim's professor, I received absolutely no word from the Dean of Students or anyone else in the administration until three days later when I received a terse note which read, "Jim Smith has withdrawn from the University. Please note whether he withdrew from your course with a Pass or a Fail."

I left teaching the next year.

Martha Ann, describing her experience as a mathematics
professor at a large southern public university

While we know that smallness alone is no guarantee of a school's educational effectiveness, we do believe that a large size is a mostly negative factor in achieving the goals of higher education. Universities are not immune from the law of decreasing return in regard to increased size. We would estimate the optimum-size undergraduate learning environment to be an academic community consisting of no more than two thousand students subdivided into English-style residential colleges of around three hundred students each. Large state universities with their dehumanizing high-rise dormitories, legions of graduate teaching assistants, and tens of thousands of undergraduates are antithetical to the pursuit of knowledge, meaning, and community. There are those who respond, "But don't many students at larger schools do quite well on standardized tests like the GRE or the LSAT?" Such arguments fail to move us. The quantification and standardization of education, represented in such tests, is precisely what we are arguing against. Even relatively small universities like Duke with 6,130 undergraduates and the University of Vermont with 7,925 are difficult to control. Viable undergraduate learning communities at the mega-universities described in chapter 5 are an almost impossible dream.

What we are proposing is downsizing colleges and universities to a more reasonable scale and eventually decoupling undergraduate education from the largest of them. Growth at universities with more than five thousand undergraduates should be brought to a halt. Proposals for new undergraduate dormitories, classroom buildings, research laboratories, computer centers, or libraries should be rigorously examined. Over the next decade, the aim of large universities should be either completely to spin off their undergraduate programs or significantly decentralize them in a manner consistent with the residential college mode. Too many of our universities resemble General Motors of the fifties. While American business has radically transformed the corporation of the fifties, the World War II–induced behemoths churning out haphazardly built, assembly line–produced vehicles, American higher education is still saddled with huge institutional relics that produce assembly-line graduates. American higher education must show some of the same creativity and courage that we have seen recently in much of American business. Downsizing is the order of the day.

The three best-known American examples of the residential college systems are Harvard, Princeton, and Yale. Yale's twelve residential colleges are self-sufficient communities within Yale College, each with its own dining hall, library, courtyard, seminar rooms, practice rooms, and numerous other facilities ranging from dark-rooms to printing presses, from game rooms to saunas. At the end of their first year, Harvard students are assigned to a house in which they will live for the remainder of their undergraduate career. Each house has a master, a senior tutor or dean, a tutorial staff, a library, and dining facilities. All houses are coeducational, and much of the social, athletic, extracurricular, and academic life at Harvard centers on the house. At Princeton all freshmen and sophomores live and dine in one of five residential colleges. A small number of juniors and seniors live and eat in the residential colleges; but most live in the upperclass dorms, and more than half dine in Princeton's well-known independent eating clubs.

In no sense are we suggesting that the residential college system as practiced by the aforementioned universities is a panacea. We know that the residential college experiments at the University of Virginia and at Princeton have had their critics. Yet we do defend the notion that size is an important issue. Even with the residential college system, size mitigates against the benefits of residential colleges when, as is the case at Harvard, there are 6,672 undergraduates dominated by 11,601 graduate students and professional students, or at Yale where there are 5,194 undergraduates out of a total enrollment of 11,129. Although Princeton, with just 4,525 under-graduates, is the smallest of the three, we have previously noted Princeton's own admission that it struggles with a destructive social environment. Middlebury College, with just 1,960 students, has attempted to emulate some aspects of the residential college system, but with only mixed success. The large student residence halls at Middlebury have been grouped into five "geographically coherent" units, each called a commons. Each commons has its own budget for social and cultural events and its own system of self-governance. Faculty and staff, as well as students, belong to the various commons units. The problem with Middlebury's commons system is that it does not go far enough in the direction of decentralized living. Although Middlebury comes close to what we consider to be the optimum-size college, most of its commons do not have their own dining facilities.

Duke has recently gone through a heated, but ultimately productive, debate on this issue. The debate has resulted in major changes in residential life there, though without taking the more drastic and expensive step of instituting residential colleges. Some schools like Duke may already have enough vibrant forms of group life to foster community through specialized selective living groups rather than through residential colleges. Spectrum House, which promotes multicultural diversity among its residents, and Roundtable, which gathers its inhabitants on the basis of their commitment to community service, are examples of Duke selective living groups attempting to carve out a manageable, intimate, focused community within a large university environment.

In California, the Claremont Colleges have brought together five contiguous undergraduate colleges that maintain their distinct identities, yet share a graduate school, a library, and other facilities. They thus maintain their small size while enjoying some of the benefits of cooperation. Perhaps this is a good model for the future.

Over the long term, during the next decade, we are proposing that large universities basically withdraw from the undergraduate teaching business. The university of the future would consist of a collection of professional schools, graduate-degree-granting programs, high-level research institutions, adult education, and professional outreach services. State universities would provide support services to a network of colleges not located on the central university campus, including administrative and financial services, library services, central computing facilities, as well as specialized courses for advanced undergraduates. Seniors in satellite colleges affiliated with the university might be allowed to take a limited number of graduate courses at the university.

Most undergraduate colleges would be liberal arts colleges. Though there is nothing to prevent establishing undergraduate business or engineering colleges, we believe that business and engineering are best taught at the graduate level by professional schools.

There are those who will cry that this is an arrogant, "elitist" proposal. They will point to the legions of students who have received a college education at our large, mostly state-run schools. They will charge that what we are proposing here will take mountains of money, huge amounts of cash, in a time when all schools, public and private, are running out of funds.

We reply that our system of higher education has already been participating in a debilitating, undemocratic elitism characterized by the gap between the student experience at the large, impersonal, public mega-university and that at the small liberal arts college. We want to see that all students, not just those with large incomes or large scholarships, have the privilege of a small, face-to-face education.

Moreover, we encourage those who charge that these proposals would be extravagantly expensive to be honest about the extravagance, the waste, and the redundancy present in the large educational institutions. For decades, principally as a result of its participation in a wartime economy, American business thought that bigness, standardization, and assembly-line production techniques saved money. In the past ten years, American business has confronted the diminishing returns in regard to size. There are some tasks, particularly those that thrive on communication, interaction, and cooperation, in which cost and efficiency decline in exact proportion to size. Downsizing is not a call to withdrawal from commitment to educate the largest possible number of qualified students, but rather an attempt to give all of our students the best possible education by the most efficient means.

To finance the shift toward decentralized liberal arts colleges, we would close many redundant state-supported professional schools and graduate programs. For many states — not including California, New York, and Texas — there is little need for multiple, state-supported medical schools, law schools, and engineering schools. This is particularly true of states like Mississippi and North Carolina that have a proliferation of state universities. These schools are testimonial more to the pride and power of their local legislators than to their educational value. For example, North Carolina struggles to support two state-owned medical schools that must compete with the well-financed private medical schools at Duke and

Wake Forest, siphoning funds from one of the worst primary and secondary state school systems in the country. Many underfinanced, undersubscribed universities should be downsized back to colleges. Having experienced a couple of decades during which numerous colleges and two-year institutions frantically moved toward pinning the name "university" upon themselves, we must now help these schools recover the dignity, the focus, and the efficiency that comes from reclaiming their identity as colleges dedicated to undergraduate education.

It is not obvious that every state needs a dental school, a veterinary school, or state-of-the-art research institutions in nuclear physics and microbiology. The cold war is over, and we do not need nearly so many nuclear physicists, mathematicians, chemists, and defense-related engineers. As taxpayers demand cutbacks in the so-called defense budget, research universities are going to discover painfully how much of their intellectual activity has been dictated by the Pentagon. A preoccupation with short-run profitability and stock prices has prompted American companies to reduce expenditures for basic research. Thus not only is there less demand for PhDs in basic science and engineering, but there is less private and government funding available to support expensive high-tech research in these fields. As the federal government returns previously federally funded programs back to the states, state governments are going to turn to their higher education budgets as sources for funds. For instance, even after a decade of cuts in the state higher education budget, the week after his inauguration, the new governor of Virginia, George F. Allen, made it clear that he would look to that state's higher education budgets as the most fruitful area for budget cuts and tax savings.[5]

Perhaps the massive cutbacks in government- and business-funded research can be seen as an opportunity, rather than an impending disaster, an externally induced invitation for us to return to the basic purposes of education. Howard University is going through

5. "Tough State-Budget Line," *Chronicle of Higher Education,* January 20, 1995, p. A23.

a time of dramatic cutbacks, firings, and retrenchment. Now, forced to make radical cuts overnight, without careful planning for the future, Howard finds it difficult to manage its misfortunes. This trauma, faced by the once-powerful and valued Howard University, whose ill-planned, governmentally induced and encouraged growth met decreasing enrollments and shrinking government subsidies, will be experienced by other institutions. Be well assured that if our faculties and administrators do not take this opportunity, we shall then be led through the humiliating process of having legislators and mere market pressures hack our schools to pieces, bit by bit.

Graduate education has always cost more than undergraduate education because of small class sizes and laboratory equipment requirements. Universities should become much more selective in choosing departments and fields in which to offer PhD degrees. The manner in which some graduate departments continue to produce PhDs in fields already oversupplied borders on the immoral. Those who would defend the mega-universities on the basis of their altruistic desire to provide the largest possible number of students with access to higher education ought honestly to examine how much potential undergraduate funding is siphoned off at these institutions by expensive, glamorous, but relatively unproductive graduate and professional programs. For too long undergraduate colleges have seen their main value as feeding their students into the university for graduate and professional work. We want to reverse that process, inviting universities to see themselves as existing for and supportive of the task of undergraduate education.

Since professors in newly emerging liberal arts colleges will not be under the university publish-or-perish mandate, they can be expected to teach more — perhaps as many as four or five courses per semester. More will be said about teachers who teach in the next chapter.

As universities begin downsizing and cutting back on their undergraduate programs, former undergraduate dormitories can either be transformed to graduate and professional dormitories or converted to apartment buildings or much-needed housing for the elderly. We see much educational value in colleges attempting to foster more interaction between the generations. Surplus under-graduate classrooms and office space may either be adapted to graduate and professional use or temporarily rented.

With modern telecommunications networks, universities may offer their satellite colleges televised courses on topics too specialized to be included in the curricula of most small colleges, such as Chinese, Japanese, advanced physics, and molecular biology. Universities might be seen as resource centers that offer support for strong undergraduate colleges, the strong undergraduate colleges being the basic units of American higher education, with the universities functioning for their support rather than as their norm to emulate.

Why should universities continue to support big-time football and basketball programs? Are the alleged sports revenues, claims of visibility, and alumni loyalty true? University stadiums and basketball field houses could be sold or rented to nearby professional teams. Wofford College has reversed the usual trend of professional teams feeding off college athletics. Wofford is allowing the Carolina Panthers football team to use its facilities as a summer practice camp, facilities that have been greatly expanded by the Panthers organization and will be used by Wofford students and faculty during the year as a campus health club. In downsizing, intercollegiate athletics would return to the scale on which it existed before World War II. Small colleges would compete among themselves for the pleasure of it, not to train professional athletes and hype alumni and state legislators. If athletic scholarships were continued, their educational usefulness, not simply their athletic value, would need to be demonstrated.

With an effective residential college system, fraternities and sororities would receive much-needed competition; they would possibly become obsolete. For decades, on many campuses, fraternities and sororities have provided a second-best alternative to the residential college system in America. In their fraternity or sorority, students found the sense of community they craved, but which the college or university failed to provide. Indeed, the very existence of the Greek system may at least partially explain why so few colleges

110

and universities have adopted the English residential college plan. In the words of Reynolds Price, present-day fraternities and sororities are "grotesque relics" of nineteenth-century college life that "have long since ceased to serve any role not better served by means less expensive, in every sense, of the university's time and life-blood. Worse, they're our main force for division and waste — waste of the crucial youth of our students and what their elders might learn from them."

Price is particularly critical of the role fraternities play in campus alcohol abuse and anti-intellectualism. Yet the positive aspect of the Greek system's resilience is its testimonial to the importance of the search for community in students' lives, even though we believe that search can be better facilitated by the creation of groups other than fraternities and sororities.

Obviously, restructuring higher education will be a long and arduous task taking several decades to complete. But just as multi-million-dollar industrial conglomerates have outlived their usefulness and have given way to more creative adaptations, so too will large mega-university degree factories. It is not by chance alone that small colleges such as Amherst, Dartmouth, Middlebury, Mount Holyoke, Smith, Vassar, Wellesley, and Williams command premium prices in the marketplace. They charge high tuition because they provide a high value-added product.

Making the Customer King

Suppose that there were no student loans and very little of any other sort of state aid to higher education; imagine that every student . . . were paying the full cost of his or her own tuition. . . . American universities teach what they do for the same reason Polish factories used to turn out pairs of boots with two left feet: because an absence of consumer sovereignty enables them to get away with it. . . . With greater sacrifices demanded of the families of those who sought higher education, the proportion of Americans going on to university would shrink. That would in turn mean that state governments could no longer count on higher education to remedy the deficiencies of high school education. America turns out students the way General Motors used to turn out cars. . . . It is sometimes thought to be a paradox that America has by far the most elaborate system of higher education in the industrialized world and among the very worst systems of primary and secondary education. In fact, the two complement each other . . . if the high schools were better, Americans could close many of their universities.[6]

By attempting to be all things to all people, large-scale universities have allowed their most important business — undergraduate education — to be seriously eroded. For too long university trustees and state legislators have been biased toward professional schools and graduate education. It is now time to turn the situation around, to recover the centrality of undergraduate education. If higher education is to survive, we must begin setting new priorities and downsizing now.

6. David Frum, *Dead Right* (New York: Basic Books, 1994), pp. 191-92.

CHAPTER 8

Teachers Who Teach

Too much of education at every level seems to be organized for the convenience of educators and the institution's interests, procedures and prestige, and too little focused on the needs of students.[1]

At many colleges and universities, it is assumed that when a freshly minted PhD arrives on the scene, he or she already knows how to teach. Nothing could be further from the truth. Where are these junior faculty members supposed to have learned how to teach?

Despite the platitudes academic administrators may utter to the contrary, teaching is not very important at most leading research universities. What matters is publishing on the current "hot topics" in the "right" academic journals in one's narrowly defined area of expertise. It matters not whether there is any relationship between what you teach and what you publish. Yet part of the rationale underlying the heavy emphasis on research is that it is supposed to strengthen one's teaching ability. Maybe, maybe not.

In a 1992 nationwide survey by the U.S. Education Depart-

1. Report of the Wingspread Group on Higher Education, *An American Imperative: Higher Expectations for Higher Education* (Racine, Wis.: Johnson Foundation, 1993), p. 13.

ment, 35 percent of faculty members who worked full time on campuses said their principal activity was something other than teaching — 12 percent listed research, 12 percent listed administrative tasks, 11 percent listed assorted other activities like clinical work and community service.[2] Just 65 percent of faculty consider teaching their principal activity.

Teaching as Serious Business

When I began teaching at Middlebury College after thirty years at Duke, I was surprised to find that I was expected to participate in a week-long orientation period to prepare me to teach at Middlebury. Faculty orientation was something unknown to me. The week began with an all-day meeting of the entire facility at Middlebury's Bread Loaf campus to discuss in considerable detail the College's strategic plan. The president presided over the meeting and discussion was led by the senior administrators of the college. When the day was over I was exhausted, but I felt like I knew what Middlebury College was all about. Later in the week I attended a meeting of new faculty members, most of whom were half my age, whose aim was to teach us how to teach Middlebury students. When classes began the following week, I was convinced that teaching is the serious business of Middlebury.[3]

Tom Naylor

---

2. *Chronicle of Higher Education,* November 23, 1994, pp. A15-A16.
3. Fortunately, Duke has now established a center for research into and improvement of undergraduate teaching in which faculty members from fourteen Duke departments receive support and encouragement for better classroom teaching. The goal of the Center for Teaching and Learning at Duke University is "to initiate within a research university a more directed effort toward understanding

Not only do most university professors teach too little, but for over thirty years high academic status has actually been associated with minimum teaching loads. The less you teach, the more prestigious your position. Of course, the ultimate form of academic recognition is to be in such a strong bargaining position that you teach nothing at all.[4] And parents wonder why the tab for college tuition keeps rising.

Tenure also works against good teaching. Tenured faculty tend to tenure clones of themselves. Those who have devalued teaching in their own careers are unlikely to tenure younger colleagues who emphasize teaching. Tenure also makes it difficult for colleges and universities to fire incompetent teachers. In no other field are professionals guaranteed lifetime employment regardless of their competence. Despite the protests of the American Association of University Professors — a group that, having forsaken its earlier noble objectives, has now contented itself with dreams of becoming a union for academics — tenure is an anachronism. Today's uncertain economy gives us the opportunity gradually to phase out the outmoded tenure system. One simply does not have to offer a professor a lifetime contract to teach when alternative forms of employment in business and government are diminishing so rapidly. Academic salaries, as well as the intrinsic benefits of college life, are high

---

the many aspects of teaching and learning." There are now more than two hundred similar teaching centers, 40 percent having been established in the last four years. We are much encouraged by this effort to do research and training in undergraduate teaching.

4. A Carnegie Foundation survey found that faculty are not forsaking teaching for research. Seventy percent of all faculty (and 33 percent of faculty at research universities) indicated that their primary interest lay in teaching rather than research. Faculty at least *say*, when asked, that teaching is important to them. However, the same study also indicated that the financial and prestige rewards are definitely tilted toward faculty who do research and who publish. One conclusion is that faculty want to give more emphasis to teaching, but institutions have not been successful in rewarding good teaching. See the summary of this research along with the thoughtful analysis by Francis Oakley in "Against Nostalgia: Reflections on Our Present Discontents in American Higher Education," in *The Politics of Liberal Education,* ed. D. J. Gless and B. H. Smith (Durham, N.C.: Duke University Press, 1992), pp. 267-89.

enough to attract first-rate college teachers without the benefit of tenure. A system of tenured employment tends to attract those who value job security and stability rather than creativity and innovation. Tenure should be replaced by renewable ten-year contracts, where the terms of renewal assume the professor maintains at least some minimum level of competence in the classroom.[5] Any well-managed college will encourage long-term stability in its faculty.

The charges of right-wing critics like Dinesh D'Souza that there is a new McCarthyism of the Left and "politically correct" coercion are considerably overdrawn.[6] Few professors take a stand on anything too controversial, even though they are fully protected by tenure. If tenure were so essential, why isn't there a broader range of political, philosophical, and theological debate on most campuses? Tenure has actually contributed to the stultifying anti-intellectual atmosphere on campus by rewarding the "living dead" with permanent employment and by intimidating younger professors into submitting themselves to the values of the older faculty in exchange for tenure.

Above all, we believe that in undergraduate colleges *all* faculty should teach. The academic class system has accentuated the gap between the teachers and nonteachers in universities. It is now time to abandon the two-tier system in which those at the very top of the academic pecking order teach little or nothing and the teaching is left to the drones who can't make it in the rarefied realms of research.

Of course, we know the typical rebuttal to these concerns: *You have confused the difference between a college and a university.* Under-

5. The future of Bennington will be a good litmus test for this proposal. Will good faculty want to teach there under contracts rather than under tenure? Of course, much depends on how well colleges other than Bennington are able to preserve their tradition of tenure despite pressures for change.

6. Dinesh D'Souza, *Illiberal Education* (New York: Free Press, 1991). See Paul Rogat Loeb's extended discussion of the "politically correct" controversy in *A Generation at the Crossroads: Apathy and Action on the American Campus* (New Brunswick, N.J.: Rutgers University Press, 1994), pp. 331-66. D'Souza makes today's faculties sound a good deal more interesting and controversial than we really are.

graduates who desire the small campus you have been describing —
the small student body, a faculty totally committed to teaching —
select a college. Those who want to sacrifice these undeniable benefits for other benefits select a university where:

- They have the opportunity to learn from faculty who are themselves generating new knowledge, who are carrying out research
  at the cutting edge of their disciplines.
- They have the opportunity to participate in advanced research
  by engaging in independent work with the professor in the
  laboratory, or by participating in the research projects of the
  professor.
- They have the opportunity to take courses, as an undergraduate,
  from faculty who teach in law, medicine, theology, and business
  schools.

Aside from the question of how many undergraduates actually
avail themselves of these university-engendered activities (we expect
no more than a very small percentage of undergraduates participate
in their professors' research activities), we believe this begs the question of what appears to happen to undergraduate teaching skills
within the context of the large university.

Our Duke colleague Stanley Hauerwas has noted that this notion of teaching as the central purpose of the university carries with
it important implications for the soul of American higher education.[7]
Hauerwas says teaching is a distinctly *moral* issue. In previous chapters of this book we have lamented higher education's denial of its
task as moral educator. The modern university likes to think of itself
as having no opinion on moral matters, as if it were morally neutral,
value-free. We merely provide our students access to certain information and then they are free to use that information in whatever
way they choose. From this unstructured curriculum the student

---

7. Stanley M. Hauerwas, "The Morality of Teaching," in *The Academic's Handbook,* ed. A. L. Deneef, C. D. Goodwin, and E. S. McCrate (Durham, N.C.: Duke Press, 1988), pp. 19-28.

learns not to insist on any value as superior to any other, not to claim that certain goods are to be valued over others. In short, says Hauerwas, "contemporary university education is an extended training in cynicism" where students receive training in how not to care about anything too strongly. Otherwise they will be accused of being narrow or closed-minded. This is called "intellectual objectivity."[8]

Yet Hauerwas would have us note that *this also is a "morality."* Perhaps it is a superficial or a cynical one, but it is a kind of morality. It is the nihilistic morality that has undercut the ethos necessary to maintain a university as an intellectual and moral community, the same sorry morality that now plagues much American business and public life.

Against this detached, cynical morality that fails to acknowledge itself as a morality, Hauerwas somewhat surprisingly calls us back to our most basic activity — teaching — claiming that the task of teaching carries with it great moral significance for the university. Unfortunately, through their formation in PhD programs, new scholars see themselves not as teachers of undergraduates but as members of a field, initiates into the guild of sociologists, or botanists, or computer scientists. They have a commitment to extend the boundaries of their discipline, but not a commitment to teach. A young scholar soon learns that this is the way he or she will be rewarded — first as a success in one's discipline and only secondarily, if at all, as a teacher. Acquiring a reputation in one's field is the only path for professional advancement.

Which of course explains why few faculty have much loyalty to the institution in which they serve. If they feel related to the university at all, it is to their individual department, those colleagues who will be responsible for tenure and advancement. Hauerwas laments that scholars, who have been given the leisure to read books,

8. Canadian theologian Douglas John Hall accuses modern universities of engendering "covert nihilism," which "practices detachment, noninvolvement, 'value-free' investigation. In universities and think-tanks, it cultivates the stance of objective research: that is, it shuns commitment. In the public sphere it translates into apathy and 'psychic numbing.'" *Professing the Faith: Christian Theology in the North American Context* (Philadelphia: Fortress, 1994), p. 384.

to write, and to do research through the material resources of the community, feel little obligation to serve the needs of that community.

College Teaching

Having been given the privilege to spend most of our lives reading books is a reminder that our task as teachers is to ensure the wisdom of our civilization by instilling in our students a passion for the examined life.

Stanley M. Hauerwas

We see ourselves as academics, not as intellectuals — as academics extending the boundaries of a discipline, adding knowledge to the field when what we ought primarily to regard ourselves as is people who teach. The argument is always, "Well, professors who do good research, who write well, and who are recognized in their field will also, quite naturally, be good teachers. Their enthusiasm for their discipline will be contagious to the students they teach."

There is some truth to this claim. Courses teaching college teachers how to teach do not excite us much. Ideally, the enthusiasm generated by our academic research should contribute to our ability to teach, but only if faculty regard teaching as more than an adjunct activity for those who can afford the time away from their study in order to be in a classroom. Tom's study of downsizing and reorganization in American business and Will's thought on Christian ethics and public life have contributed, we believe, to the substance and energy of our classroom teaching. Teaching is the point of it all.

Many claim that research can enhance our classroom teaching. But it also ought to be said that classroom teaching can contribute to the growth of our understanding of our academic discipline. Hauerwas rightly notes that, despite the values of our research in-

119

terests, when we confine ourselves to our "discipline," that narrow range of specialized interest in which we have attained some recognition from those in that field, we become oblivious to the limits of our discipline. Our main conversations are with our colleagues in our discipline, so our conversations become narrow and uncritical. One of the great gifts of a university is colleagues — other scholars who do not share our "field," those to whom we must explain ourselves, justify our interests, and engage in conversation.

President David Davenport of Pepperdine University has attempted to move his faculty away from the old teaching-versus-research conundrum and speak instead about the need for "student learning" as the university's goal. Davenport notes that in Pepperdine's science departments, where faculty are encouraged to do their research with students and to jointly publish their results, research can be a vital part of student learning.

Students are also colleagues. If we faculty can restrain ourselves from intimidating our students by flexing our expertise in a field, our students have much to teach us through their skepticism about our enthusiasms for a subject, their fresh points of view, their questions, and their experiences. We have been advocating a new stress upon teaching as a great need of the students, but here we are stressing teaching as a requisite for the development of the various academic disciplines of the faculty.

Teaching Is Primary

We have Nobel prize–winning professors teaching common core courses. They love interacting with students and it keeps the students really excited about their studies.[9]

---

9. Christopher Brown, University of Chicago freshman, as quoted in the *Duke Chronicle*, May 26, 1994, p. 8.

Hauerwas — who teaches ministers, and sometimes doctors and lawyers — thinks it important that college teachers remind themselves that they are a *profession*. That is, teachers work together to respond to basic human need; just as doctors attempt to meet human needs in medicine, "so teaching is a way to enhance our society through knowledge and wisdom. The moral authority of the teacher derives from this commitment and is the reason why the society as a whole feels betrayed when it is not honored." Students remind us that the goal of teaching a subject like literary criticism is not to produce a future generation of literary critics — who needs that? Our goal must not be the production of mere clones of ourselves. The goal of classes in literary criticism is to produce better people, folk who are rendered into better human beings through the insights and critical skills gained in the practices engendered by literary criticism.

Thus, Hauerwas wants us faculty to own up to the truth that we are all moral educators. We are not neutral. Anytime we stand up in a classroom and teach, we are doing more than merely laying out information; we are substantially shaping the moral life of our students. Whenever we ask an economics major to read a novel, we are making a kind of moral statement, attempting to form that student into a peculiar kind of person.

Moral Examples

The failure of the modern university is not that those teaching in it fail to shape students morally, but that we fail to take responsibility for doing so. . . . There is no way as teachers we can or should avoid being moral examples for our students.

Stanley M. Hauerwas

When students take a course because of the professor teaching it rather than the subject being taught, they show that they instinctively know what is really going on in education, namely, the exemplification of certain patterns, skills, practices, and convictions in the lives of those who teach. "I think students are right to want to learn from those who manifest in their lives the lessons they have learned from their scholarship," says Hauerwas.

Thus one of our colleagues, a distinguished research chemist, once commented that he felt today's students could benefit from the ethics of chemists. *"The ethics of chemists?"* I asked in confusion.

"Sure, the ethics of chemists. There is no way to be a good chemist and to be a liar. The ethical virtues of honesty about results, openness with one's colleagues, consistency in method are all among the ethics of chemists."

You can imagine why this colleague's undergraduate course on "Science for Non-Scientists" is a great success at our university.

A good teacher has enough confidence in the ultimate human value of his or her discipline not to mind changing other people's lives for the sake of it. Great courage is required to be a good teacher, the courage born out of the conviction that if our students will read these books, will learn these skills, will adopt these scholarly disciplines, they will become better persons in the process. All of us professors are producers of character, whether we like it or not.

Faculty enjoy thinking of themselves as powerless people. But few people are more powerful than those who shape the hearts, minds, and actions of others. There is simply no way for faculty to sidestep debates over what sort of persons we hope to produce through our teaching. To fail to have this debate about the ends of our colleges and universities is irresponsibly to refuse to acknowledge the moral implications of what we are doing.

Academic Assessment

The sad fact is that campuses spend far more time and money establishing the credentials of applicants than they do assessing the knowledge, skills, and competencies of their graduates.

Indeed, the entire system is skewed in favor of the input side of the learning equation: credit hours, library collections, percentage of faculty with terminal degrees, and the like. The output side of the equation — student achievement — requires much greater attention than it now receives. That attention should begin by establishing improved measures of student achievement, measures that are credible and valued by the friends and supporters of education, by testing and accrediting bodies and by educational institutions themselves.[10]

If college faculty began teaching four or five courses each semester rather than only two or three, not only would the cost per student decline but the quality of teaching might actually improve with experience. Some professors teach so little that they never properly hone their underdeveloped teaching skills. Forced to teach more, professors might receive added encouragement to join with others in team teaching. When Tom approached Will about the need for an undergraduate course in "The Search for Meaning" and Will pleaded that he didn't have time because of administrative and research responsibilities, Tom's proposal for a team-taught course not only enabled the course to happen but also led to increased interaction between two disparate disciplines.

If undergraduate education is restructured into a system of smaller colleges with greater emphasis on teaching, then a plethora

10. *An American Imperative,* p. 15.

of options become available to make the classroom come alive, including more seminars, team teaching, interdisciplinary courses, small-group experiences, and tutorials. Smaller classes and seminars are more participatory than large lecture courses. The most effective learning environment comprises three-way interaction among individual students, other students in the classroom, and the professor. Students should be encouraged to take ownership and be actively involved in their own education. Professors serve as mentors, instructors, coaches, facilitators, and guides. Students should function as active workers as well as learners.

Technology can be a powerful classroom tool — particularly audiovisual equipment that enables the professor to introduce film, videos, music, art, and photography into the class. We are less convinced of the merits of computer-assisted instruction. In general, colleges and universities have been oversold on personal computers and connected campuses. It is not uncommon to find rooms full of desktop computers on college campuses that, for the most part, are being used almost exclusively for word processing or e-mail conversations with friends on other campuses. Glorified typewriters is what they are. Why do universities feel obliged to spend such huge sums of money on PCs?

In rendering library research into a high-tech matter of punching a few buttons and watching the computer search data bases for you, student research has become a quick trip to the computer. As we have previously noted, today's college students have too much free time — not too little. Is it possible that modern technology has contributed to the anti-intellectual campus atmosphere by giving students even more free time to party than might otherwise have been the case?

One of our objectives in decentralizing undergraduate education into residential colleges is to enhance student-faculty interaction outside of the classroom — particularly in residence halls. There should be one or two faculty members physically living within each residential college consisting of no more than three hundred students. These faculty members, along with a student-elected advisory council, should organize residential college seminars, lectures, discussions, and short courses. Out-of-class learning experiences should be available not only on weeknights but also on the weekends so that those who do not wish to party all weekend have a positive alternative available to them.

Residential faculty members should eat one or two meals each day in the residential dining hall and be available to students for informal discussions and counseling. There should be some seminar rooms in the residential colleges where regular courses can be offered either in the daytime or evening.

Many colleges and universities begin virtually no classes before 9:00 A.M. Saturday classes simply do not exist. As a result, expensive classroom space is underutilized, putting pressure on universities for unnecessary additional buildings.

We feel that the way to address campus alcohol abuse is not by imposing additional bureaucratic rules on students but rather by creating a better learning atmosphere, increasing academic demands, and reducing some of the freedom available to students — for example, the luxury of no Saturday classes and no eight o'clock classes. Spending only about 15 hours in class and 150 hours out of class, students have more free time than they can productively consume.

The permissive atmosphere that has evolved on college campuses over the past twenty years has resulted in too little teaching, too little learning, too many choices, too much partying, at too high a cost to students, parents, and society as a whole.

Alas, there is little evidence to suggest that academic administrators possess either the will or the ability to turn the situation around. If the learning environment on college campuses is to improve, the faculty must assume the power and the responsibility to invoke fundamental changes in the academy. These matters are too important to be left to university administrators or student-life bureaucrats. By offering to teach more and to make themselves more available to students, professors can provide the necessary leadership to reinvigorate undergraduate education. We professors are not "academics," those who have become adept at manipulating the current system of higher education to our own advantage in securing a permanent place for ourselves in the system. We are *teachers*, those who initiate students into those skills that are necessary for them to be lifetime learners.

Over the past twenty years, colleges have become dens of hedonism where students amuse themselves for four years before confronting the workplace, graduate school, or professional school — a "last adolescent hurrah before a lifetime of career hell," was how one cynical undergraduate put it. The permissive campus atmosphere created by faculty members whose aim was to keep students off their backs has not been conducive to good teaching or good scholarship. It is time for the faculty to assume the primary leadership role in transforming undergraduate colleges into communities of teachers and scholars. We must not abdicate our responsibility to serve the social order through sustained discussion of what is good, what is true, and what is beautiful.

Some of our institutions and the people who practice our profession have stretched the public's ability to believe that our institutions exist to serve their needs.[11]

Colleges and universities are worth preserving, are worthy of the incredible expenditure of human and material resources, only if we teach.

11. Duke President Nannerl O. Keohane, in *The Duke Dialogue*, April 21, 1995, p. 5.

CHAPTER 9

Curriculum Counterrevolution

*The simple fact is that some faculties and institutions certify
for graduation too many students who cannot read and write
very well, too many whose intellectual depth and breadth are
unimpressive, and too many whose skills are inadequate in the
face of the demands of contemporary life.[1]*

We really believe that college is mostly about people — colleagues, students, and faculty living and working together —
from which the very name "college" is derived. However, these
colleagues have their life together structured in a certain way. Thus
we close with a brief consideration of curriculum reform. Part of us
believes that the most important curriculum reform is to ensure that
a college or university has good people teaching good students good
classes. The people are the curriculum. In fact, sometimes we have
been guilty, in American higher education, of attempting to solve
our problems with people by tinkering with the curriculum. Extensive curriculum reform is no substitute for close attention to the
character of the faculty, the composition of the student body, and

1. Report of the Wingspread Group on Higher Education, *An American
Imperative: Higher Expectations for Higher Education* (Racine, Wis.: Johnson Foundation, 1993), p. 1.

the quality of their interaction. However, concern about curriculum has its place in the reform of higher education.[2]

It is our belief that American college students take too few courses, and that many of these are frivolous and based on minimum intellectual content, thus providing students with too much free time to engage in destructive social behavior. As a result, students and their parents realize a relatively poor return on their increasingly high investment in higher education. As part of a renewed commitment to undergraduate teaching, faculties must courageously grapple with curriculum reform.

Never before in the history of the world has a society attempted to make higher education available to so many students from such a diversity of backgrounds. An explosion of college students that began in the 1950s came close to quadrupling between 1960 and 1980. Today, more than 60 percent of our high school graduates can be expected, at some point in their lives, to enroll in college. American higher education has shifted from training a class of elite professionals to the demanding endeavor of educating the masses.[3] This admirable diversity makes curriculum oversight increasingly important. Large numbers of our students come to college unprepared for the rigors of advanced intellectual work. Particularly in the first years of college, curriculum is a means of insuring that each student quickly reaches his or her learning potential, mastering the basics in order to move into advanced thinking.

2. "In the twentieth century the curriculum fell apart. . . . The death of the classical course of study opened the way to a curriculum burdened with such diversity of purpose, style, and institutional form that the word *curriculum* became a concept of convenience rather than precision." Frederick Rudolph, *Curriculum: A History of the American Undergraduate Course of Study Since 1636* (San Francisco: Jossey-Bass, 1977), p. 245. Rudolph's is the best work we have on the story of the curriculum disarray that plagues our colleges and universities.

3. Francis Oakley, "Against Nostalgia: Reflections on Our Present Discontents in American Higher Education," in *The Politics of Liberal Education*, ed. D. J. Gless and B. H. Smith (Durham, N.C.: Duke University Press, 1992), p. 283.

The Reinvention of Higher Education

What does society want from higher education? We need for higher education to reinvent itself, particularly in regard to undergraduate education.[4]

While the diversity of American higher educational institutions demands much local adaptation and creativity in order to address the specific needs of students at each institution, we believe there is value in proposing a basic undergraduate curriculum. To improve undergraduate higher education we propose a core curriculum consisting of twenty required academic courses, twenty-one elective courses, and eight physical education courses. Students would be expected to take five academic courses plus one physical education course each semester throughout the duration of their four-year college stay. This does not mean that we are first forced to resolve all of our intellectual disagreements, to uniformly affirm some "common culture," some form of the "Western canon" that we must push on our students. A lively faculty is a faculty full of conflicts, rich with a diversity of voices. The content of the curriculum can be shaped by those voices.[5] A cacophony of faculty voices is not detrimental to undergraduate education if there is much faculty-student interaction.

The Uneducated Graduate

A 1992 analysis of college transcripts by the U.S. Department of Education revealed that 26.2 percent of recent

4. Charles Bray, of the Robert Wood Johnson Foundation, quoted in the *Durham Herald-Sun,* January 9, 1994, p. G3.
5. See Gerald Graff, "Teach the Conflicts," in *Politics of Liberal Education,* pp. 57-74.

bachelor's degree recipients earned not a single under-graduate credit in history; 30.8 percent did not study mathematics of any kind; 39.6 percent earned no credits in either English or American literature; and 58.4 percent left college without any exposure to foreign language. Much too frequently, American higher education now offers a smorgasbord of fanciful courses in a fragmented curriculum that accords as much credit for "Introduction to Tennis" and for courses in pop culture as it does for "Principles of English Composition," history, or physics, thereby trivializing education — indeed, misleading students by implying that they are receiving the education they need for life when they are not.[6]

The Search for Meaning

During the first semester of a student's first year in college we would recommend a seminar on "The Search for Meaning" similar to the one currently taught at Duke, Middlebury, the University of Vermont, and a few other places. (See Appendix.) The aim of such a seminar would be to provide a conceptual framework and a process to facilitate the search for meaning that attempts to integrate the spiritual, intellectual, emotional, and physiological dimensions of life. The course encourages students to review their life *histories;* come to terms with *meaninglessness* in their lives; confront *separation* from themselves and others; contemplate the consequences of a life based merely upon *having;* seek meaning through *being;* and formulate a *personal strategy* to address the most important quest human beings face — the need for their lives to have enduring meaning. Tools for the search include philosophy, religion, psychotherapy, literature, and fine arts. Coming early in the student's college career, the course encourages the student to take active responsibility for his or her

6. *An American Imperative*, p. 5.

education. With a student expected to have four to six different careers in a lifetime, we believe there is a strong case for a broad-based, liberal arts education with stress upon learning the skills of adaptation, planning, and personal responsibility for one's education.

English Composition

First-year students must also take a course in English composition and pass an English proficiency examination before being allowed to enter the second year of college. This two-hour examination shall consist of writing an original essay comparing two contrasting essays on the same subject that the student has read. The student's essay shall be evaluated by a team of professors according to a number of criteria including content, style, spelling, grammar, originality, critical insight, and overall writing ability.

The Literacy Gap

The literacy of college graduates is "less than impressive" at best and "near alarming" at worst, say the authors of a report sponsored by the Educational Testing Service. . . . Only 11 per cent of the graduates of four-year colleges scored at the highest level of prose literacy. . . . Only 4 per cent of the graduates of two-year colleges performed at that level.

The literacy study tested adults on specific tasks. To score at the highest level of prose literacy, for example, one would have to be able to write a brief essay contrasting the perspectives of the authors of two stories about childhood.

College graduates outperformed people with only a high-school education, but not always by much.[7]

7. *Chronicle of Higher Education,* December 14, 1994, p. A39.

Good writing involves the skills required to think well. Without acquisition of the thought skills required for good composition, students are unable to move forward as competent thinkers.

Mathematics

Every college graduate should be able to demonstrate at least a minimum level of competency in mathematics. We recommend an introductory course in calculus or a course in statistical inference and data analysis. Calculus has become an important prerequisite for courses in chemistry, physics, engineering, and economics. A grasp of the relationship between statistical inference and the scientific method is fundamental to an understanding of the physical and social sciences. Even for students who will never pursue a career directly related to mathematics, statistics and data analysis have become essential requirements for educated adults. Many college students may have to take a remedial mathematics course for which no credit would be given prior to taking the aforementioned two required courses.

The Core Curriculum

Number of Courses	Courses
1	The Search for Meaning
1	English Composition
1	Mathematics
4	Foreign Language
2	Literature
2	History
1	Philosophy
1	Religion
2	Basic Science
2	Social Science
2	Fine Arts

8	Physical Education
21	Electives
48	
	Senior-Year Thesis

Foreign Language

In today's interdependent world the ability to communicate in some language other than one's own is of critical importance. Therefore, we recommend that college graduates successfully complete at least four courses in a foreign language or pass an equivalency examination. One of the ways in which colleges may choose to differentiate themselves from others is by the menu of foreign languages offered. No doubt French, Spanish, and German will be widely available. Colleges hoping to attract students who will later go to Jewish or Christian seminaries may offer courses in Latin, Greek, and Hebrew. For those preparing for careers in international trade, courses in Chinese, Japanese, and Russian may have appeal. African-Americans and others hoping better to understand the emerging nations of Africa may have interest in learning various African dialects. In addition to the base languages offered by a college, the range of foreign language options can be significantly broadened at a reasonable cost through telecommunications hookups with one or more universities. Today's colleges talk much about "cultural diversity." The one sure way truly to appreciate another culture is to learn that culture's language and literature.

Foreign Language

Proficiency in a second language will no longer be a degree requirement at the University of Vermont. . . . By a close vote, the faculty of UVM's College of Arts and Sciences chose between two proposals on a special ballot, either of which would have struck the requirement that students take four semesters of a second language. . . . The change will almost certainly mean job losses among the non-tenured faculty in language departments. . . . "It's a shame. It should be part of anyone's education," said Meredith Pepper, a sophomore from Atlanta who is almost finished with her fourth semester of Hebrew at UVM in preparation for study in Israel.[8]

Literature

In a sense, arguments about curriculum are arguments among faculty and students over which texts ought to be read by educated people. Through literature, our lives are broadened, we learn to see as we have not seen before, we enter the minds of others, and a mirror is held up to our deepest selves. The recent debate over the so-called canon of great literature is helpful. We agree with those who feel that we must work with a broad, diverse understanding of "great" literature. People are being formed through the literature they read.

Literary Guidance

[S]tudents have powerful images of what a perfect body is and pursue it incessantly. But deprived of literary guidance, they no longer have any image of a perfect soul, and hence do not long to have one. They do not even imagine that there is such a thing.[9]

8. *Burlington Free Press,* February 15, 1994.
9. Allan Bloom, *The Closing of the American Mind* (New York: Simon and Schuster, 1987), p. 67.

History

As we noted earlier, Neil Postman says that, in a sense, all teachers are teachers of history, those who introduce students to what humankind has learned in the past. We live in an ahistorical culture in which an ignorance of the past hinders our ability to change and to move forward into the future. Lacking knowledge of humanity's options, knowledge that is gained in great part from history, our present imagination shrinks. History enables us to enter the future much wiser than we would be if left to our own devices. In the last two decades we have discovered how limited some of our grasp of history has been. We need to listen to a wider array of voices from the past, particularly to those voices that have been excluded from academic scrutiny by historiography that attends to the history of the most powerful and vocal.

Philosophy and Religion

Too few undergraduates are exposed to the views of the world's great philosophers and the beliefs of the principal religions of the world. Educated people are those who know how to think well, who can sustain an argument, who know those who have given their lives in the search for human understanding.

Nowhere does our western, industrialized narrowness seem more pronounced than in our ignorance of religion.[10] Among other things, religion is a way of knowing, a means of being in the world through which millions have lived and which millions still live and die for.

10. For an account of the ways in which religion has been excluded from academic environments, see George M. Marsden, *The Soul of the University* (New York: Oxford University Press, 1994). See also Douglas Sloan, *Faith and Knowledge: Mainline Protestantism and American Higher Education* (Louisville: Westminster/ John Knox Press, 1995).

Basic Science

All too many college students leave the academy without any training in basic science — biology, chemistry, or physics. It should not be possible to graduate without two courses in basic science. Some colleges may want to offer one-semester survey courses in these fields. However, much can be said for a two-semester sequence in only one field in which students explore it in enough depth, including laboratory experience, that they begin to become part of the complex of practices, skills, and insights of that field.

Social Science

In no area is "course sprawl" more conspicuous than in the social sciences — psychology, anthropology, economics, political science, and sociology. Even though the idea will meet with great resistance from the respective disciplines, we believe that a strong case can be made for consolidating the course offerings in these five fields into a single department — social science.

Take economics, for example. At the heart of economics are two interdependent sets of theories — microeconomics and macro-economics. Virtually every other course offered in economics departments is merely an application of these two theories to international trade, economic development, government regulation, managerial economics, labor, monetary policy, and comparative economics. Most of what is taught in undergraduate economics courses could be compressed into no more than four courses. We believe the same is true in anthropology, political science, and sociology.

However, we still recommend two social science courses for college certification — probably survey courses in two of the afore-mentioned disciplines.

Fine Arts

Art is a principal means of apprehending the world, of exploring the self, of creating beauty out of the stuff of the world. A college graduate can hardly claim to be fully educated without some knowledge and appreciation of art, music, drama, and film. Therefore, we recommend two courses in fine arts as an important part of the core curriculum.

The National Adult Literacy Survey

According to the 1993 National Adult Literacy Survey (NALS), surprisingly large numbers of college graduates are unable, in everyday situations, to use basic skills involving reading, writing, computation, and elementary problem-solving.

The NALS tasks required participants to do three things: read and interpret prose, such as newspaper articles, work with documents like bus schedules and tables and charts, and use elementary arithmetic to solve problems involving, for example, the costs of restaurant meals or mortgages. The NALS findings were presented on a scale from low (Level 1) to high (Level 5) in each of three areas.

- in working with documents, only eight percent of college graduates reached the highest level;
- in terms of their ability to work with prose, only 10 percent of graduates were found in Level 5; and
- with respect to quantitative skills, only 12 percent of college graduates reached the highest level.

In fact, only one-half of the graduates were able to demonstrate intermediate levels of competence in each of the three areas. In the area of quantitative skills, for example, 56.3 percent of American-born, college graduates

137

were unable *consistently* to perform simple tasks, such as calculating the change from $3.00 after buying a 60 cent bowl of soup and a $1.95 sandwich.[11]

Physical Education

Under our plan for restructuring higher education, big-time, semi-professional intercollegiate athletics would be scaled back to a size commensurate with small liberal arts colleges. However, we would substantially encourage physical education as an integral part of the core curriculum. Students would be required to take one course in physical education each semester over the four years they are in college. These courses should contain a balanced mixture of health education, physical fitness exercises, and the playing of sports. Through participation in sport, in developing habits of good health, students would gain a considerably expanded notion of what it means to be "intellectual." Being intellectual is not only a matter of discipline and development of the mind but also of disciplined and intelligent development of the body. The alcohol abuse and sleep deprivation that characterize student life at many campuses indicate that attention needs to be given to physical development.[12]

Electives

In addition to the twenty required academic courses and the eight physical education courses, college graduates should take twenty-one

11. *An American Imperative,* pp. 5-6.
12. A recent study at George Washington University shows a positive correlation between a student's active involvement in the planning and direction of the class, as well as participation in extracurricular activities, and the student's academic performance. Todd M. Davis and Patricia H. Murrell, *Turning Teaching into Learning: The Role of Student Responsibility in the Collegiate Experience,* Higher Education Reports, George Washington University, Washington, D.C., 20036.

electives. Students should also be required to declare a major field of study, but may not take more than six courses in any field. To graduate, a student must submit a senior thesis and defend it in an oral examination. Admittedly, supervision of a senior thesis would require a massive amount of faculty time in those institutions that have no such practice. However, the close, sustained interaction between faculty and students involved in preparing the thesis would be a wonderful way for faculty to monitor the success or failure of their teaching efforts as well as a significant time for evaluation and reflection on the student's part as the student prepares to graduate.

Senior-Year Thesis

There ought to be an extended opportunity for students to demonstrate, toward the end of their undergraduate years, what they have learned in a coherent, sustained way. A senior-year thesis would enable students to integrate their diverse knowledge and to have the satisfaction of engaging in advanced research. Supervision of the senior thesis would also give faculty the opportunity for one last face-to-face engagement with students. The thesis would demonstrate to both faculty and students what was being accomplished through the curriculum and what changes were needed.

Preprofessional

For undergraduates aspiring to professional training in business, engineering, law, medicine, or divinity, it may make sense to give college credit for their first year in professional school, thus reducing their stay on the college campus to three years rather than four. In order to satisfy all of the undergraduate college requirements in three years, it may be necessary for a student to take an overload some semesters or to attend summer school.

It has always been possible to complete a college degree in three years at most colleges and universities by combining extra courses with summer study. Middlebury College and other places have begun marketing three-year degree programs more aggressively as a cost-reduction strategy.

The Age of Indifference

In July 1988, Gallup and the National Geographic Society announced that Americans eighteen to twenty-four years old ranked last among their peers of nine nations in their ability to locate on a map places like France, Britain, Japan, Central America. . . . A June 1990 Times Mirror study, *The Age of Indifference,* concluded that young Americans knew far less than their counterparts coming of age from the 1940s through the early 1970s, and less than older Americans. . . . Regular newspaper readership, the study found, had dropped precipitously among eighteen- to twenty-nine-year-olds from nearly 70 percent in 1965 to 30 percent in 1990. Viewership of television news dropped as well, from 52 to 41 percent.[13]

We repeat our opening caveat: In no way will tinkering with the curriculum alone change American higher education. Sometimes we have been guilty of refurbishing the curriculum because that was much easier than addressing tough personnel matters in the faculty. A new curriculum, administered by faculty with the same old attitudes, will be little innovation at all. Rather, a new curriculum (which, as you can see, is in many ways a return to an old curriculum) can be an important means of signaling to faculty and students where the college or university means to be moving.

13. Paul Rogat Loeb, *A Generation at the Crossroads: Apathy and Action on the American Campus* (New Brunswick, N.J.: Rutgers University Press, 1994), p. 69.

As we implied earlier, a curriculum is a moral matter, a statement by faculty that we have definite notions about the nature of educated women and men, and an owning by the faculty of our responsibility for the formation of those to whom this society shall look for direction in the future. We must recover the insight of John Dewey, the great educational pragmatist, who taught that all education is "public" education in that all education ought to be open to public scrutiny and ought to provide people with resources for reflection on and transformation of their world.

Frederick Rudolph closes his monumental history of the undergraduate curriculum in the United States by calling us to account for the sort of human beings our curriculum is helping to create:

> College and university faculties, strongly oriented toward their academic disciplines and wedded to the mystique of scientific investigation and suspended judgment, are not a likely source of encouragement for any renewal of concern with values and character. Even the coaches have let us down. . . . Can there be any question about the values a college or university teaches when it says: "We don't care what courses you take; you can have a B.A., and not know how to write, how to understand nuclear fission, look at a painting, or listen to music"?
>
> . . . If there are not sufficient jobs available to justify an endless production of proficient technicians . . . perhaps we can stop making technicians and get back to the business of making human beings. The time may be at hand when a reevaluation of academic purpose and philosophy will encourage the curricular developments that will focus on the lives we lead, their quality, the enjoyment they give us, and the wisdom with which we lead them. . . . And perhaps, once more, the idea of an educated person will have become a usable ideal.[14]

14. Rudolph, pp. 288-89.

CHAPTER 10

Learning Communities

"Are you all right?" one of the boys asked the sophomore girl who was lying on her back with her arms outstretched, almost like a cross. . . . It was a balmy fall afternoon in 1967. Two hours earlier, right after lunch, a group of students, all white, had loaded into a rickety Volkswagen bus with a Florida license plate. When they couldn't pull another one in, three others followed in a car. They had driven west on state highway 74, then turned north onto a county road after they crossed the Tobesofkee Creek and finally up a wagon road left by timber cutters. They stopped in a clearing where the creek did a dogleg bend. . . . "I'm fixing to be [high]," [said one of the students], pulling a small package tucked underneath his shirt and passing it around.

The girl lying on the ground has been one of the more frolicsome ones since they arrived, wading in the water, making mud pies, making up limericks. When she fell she was struggling to form her body into a triskelion. When she grabbed her second leg, and there was no third one to grab, she fell.

"She must be a philosophy major," someone said. Everyone laughed.[1]

1. Will D. Campbell, *The Stem of Jesse: The Costs of Community at a 1960s Southern School* (Macon, Ga.: Mercer University Press, 1995), pp. 153-54.

142

When Duke's West Campus was built, after the generous gift of James B. Duke, it was conceived of as an "academic village" where gymnasia, laboratories, classrooms, libraries, a chapel, and dining halls would all be interlocked in a unified college community. This arrangement signifies in an architectural way that which ought to be the norm for our life together. There is no intellectual life that is not lived in community. No scholar is a self-made woman or man.[2]

Ultimately, what seems to be missing on most college campuses is a strong sense of community among students, among faculty, and between students and faculty — a sense of belonging and connectedness. Academic life is not a solitary, inner existentialist quest for learning. It demands a journey outward as well. Nobody is a "self-made" person. Both students and faculty are haunted by an ever-present longing for community — an irresistible need for communication with each other. In our classes and conversations with today's students, we have found them amazingly willing to listen, even eager for adult interaction. Perhaps this is because, as members of the "abandoned generation," they welcome more direction and encouragement than they have previously received from their parents. In short, they long for community.[3]

2. "The primary task of higher education is to avoid the split between talk about personal growth and finding ourselves, on the one hand, and attention to the cognitive, structural, and systemic dimensions of learning on the other. Concern about the identification and cultivation of authentic and enriched selfhood, and concern about corporate life and public achievements, are not mutually exclusive alternatives. Selfhood has both private and public meanings; education has both curricular and extracurricular elements. All of these must interface in an adequate educational experience." Edward LeRoy Long, Jr., *Higher Education as a Moral Enterprise* (Washington, D.C.: Georgetown University Press, 1992), p. 26.

3. See *Campus Life: In Search of Community,* A Report by the Carnegie Foundation for the Advancement of Teaching (Princeton, N.J.: Princeton University Press, 1990). See also the extended discussion of campus community in Long, chap. 4.

Newman on the Idea of a University as Community

A University is, according to the usual designation, an Alma Mater, knowing her children one by one, not a foundry or a mint, or a treadmill.[4]

In the faculty newsletter section in the October 30, 1992, *Duke Dialogue,* Jane Tompkins, of the Duke Department of English, confessed, "I crave a sense of belonging, the feeling that I'm part of an enterprise larger than myself, part of a group that shares some common purpose." She reported that loneliness is a major factor of life for many university faculty.

Professor Tompkins says that "deliberate attention to quality of life and workplace . . . is missing from most universities I have known, and especially, a consciousness of how important it is to establish and maintain good human relations among people who occupy common space." She complains that the value structure of faculties discourages a "communal atmosphere."

"At schools that emphasize research (and this is by now a familiar story), each professor is an entrepreneur whose aim is to enhance his or her reputation within a subfield, so that he or she can move up the ladder — receive more money, more recognition, a lighter teaching load, and various other perks. In this kind of competitive, hierarchical system, people's energy naturally goes into their publications and not toward the institution or each other."

She laments that "there's no time for just hanging out."

"One might argue that the professoriate is made up largely of people who do best when left alone to pursue their own ends, and were attracted to the profession for that reason, in which case my discomfort may be anomalous."

4. John Henry Cardinal Newman, *The Idea of a University: Defined and Illustrated* (London: Longmans Green, 1896), p. 144.

Comparing universities to corporations, and praising corporations for the strides they have made in recent years in addressing issues related to the quality of life in the workplace, Professor Tompkins says "universities are every bit as product-oriented as businesses. Teaching and publishing are the products and universities pay attention to them. . . . Not much thought is given to what business people call 'product capability,' that which enables production to take place in the first place, the processes and structures that facilitate and house productive action. In simpler language, how to address human needs for nurture and support."

She ends her article with a straightforward series of suggestions.

"How can these obstacles be overcome? By a commitment to finding a community of like-minded people, by a willingness to pay the price in personal advancement and scholarly achievement as these things are now measured, by constructing an alternate reward system.

"Universities, it seems to me, should model something for students besides the ideal of individual excellence — the Olympic pole-vaulter making it over the bar. They should model social excellence as well as personal achievement, teach, by the very way they conduct their own internal business, something about our dependence upon and need for one another; something about how to achieve the feelings of acceptance and encouragement that community life affords, the sense of self-worth and belonging that keeps us all going on the inside. If institutions that purport to educate young people don't embody society's cherished ideals — community, cooperation, harmony, love — then what young people will learn will be the standards the institutions do embody: competition, hierarchy, busyness, and isolation."

Although we are all drawn to Tompkins's idyllic dream of community, few of us have experienced real community in the academy. What is community? How do we know whether a particular college is a community or not? *A community is a partnership of people committed to the care and nurturing of each other's mind, body, heart, and soul through participatory means.*[5]

---

5. Thomas H. Naylor, William H. Willimon, and Magdalena R. Naylor, *The Search for Meaning* (Nashville: Abingdon, 1994), p. 128.

145

Even though college faculty and students have endless opportunity to form communities, few of these alliances establish genuine learning communities in which there is real communication between students and faculty and the sense of commitment among members.[6]

At least in principle, it is possible for any college or university to become a community. In practice this seldom happens. Why are there so few learning communities on college campuses? What is required for a college to evolve into a community? What are the criteria for community?

The ultimate test of whether or not a college or a university is a community is *whether students and faculty are seriously concerned about each other's well-being*.

Sociologist Peter Berger once spoke of the emergence of "lifestyle enclaves" in modern America as substitutes for true community as we had once known it. In the lifestyle enclave, members are drawn together on the basis of shared interest. There is little struggle with another's intellectual, emotional, physical, or spiritual well-being; rather, lifestyle enclave members happen to be into some experience or need that periodically assembles them. "The Greek Community," "The International Community," "The African-American Community," "The Art Community," and "The Women's Community" are examples of lifestyle enclaves found on college campuses. By calling virtually every student gathering a "community," we are saved from the search for a true learning community.

Academic institutions have always stood at the gate between the past and the future, usually preparing the next generation of leaders for a world that will be new culturally and technologically. American institutions of higher learn-

---

6. Clark Kerr ridiculed calls for community on campus as mere "cries that call backward to a smaller, simpler world" unsuited to the greater purposes of a university, which are, in Kerr's words, "to bigness, to specialization, to diffusion of interests, to possibilities." We disagree. Quoted by Long, p. 46.

ing today, however, are among the more conservative forces in our society, continuing to educate in a hierarchical, individualistic, and passive manner out of tune with our society's growing need to create learning communities in every area of business, government, and social services.[7]

Do faculty really care about whether or not students have a good learning experience at college? Or are students just useful fronts to legitimatize the faculty's relatively freewheeling lifestyle of teaching, research, writing, and consulting? Do students care about what they learn, or is a college degree merely a ticket to graduate school, professional school, or a good job? Are individual students concerned only about their own grades or do they have genuine empathy for other students who may find learning to be difficult? Or is the real purpose of college life to entertain students for four years before they enter the workforce?

Shared values and *common aims* are important characteristics of college learning communities. But are the narcissism and hedonism — so prevalent in college social fraternities and sororities — sufficient to sustain true community? Or does the survival of learning communities depend on better values such as intelligence, integrity, cooperation, trust, and human empathy? The integration of such values into the lifestyle of a college group may be an arduous process. There are no shortcuts to community. We all say we want community, but do we want to risk the time and energy that communities require?

7. Eileen Moran Brown, "Contributed Essay," in the Report of the Wingspread Group on Higher Education, *An American Imperative: Higher Expectations for Higher Education* (Racine, Wis.: Johnson Foundation, 1993), p. 58.

Learning Communities

America's future will be shaped by those who are today learning how to create self-directed teams, how to make partnerships, how to work through the miscommunications and the conflicts that arise from diversity, and how to fashion a love for excellence and lifelong learning. Entrepreneurial groups within more traditional enterprises, collaborative task forces across departments, companies, industries, and even countries are all signs of the times that are coming. What they have in common is the need for people who know how to form, participate in, and lead learning communities. Colleges cannot hope to produce such people with the level of consistency and excellence they profess in every other area of their mission unless they themselves restructure. This is the task of our generation.[8]

Real communities are concerned with being — not having. Their members are committed to sharing, caring, and participating rather than owning, manipulating, controlling, and possessing. Open *communication* and *commitment* to the shared values and common purposes of individual members are critical to the stability of learning communities. Community survival depends heavily on the ability of students and faculty to extend themselves to each other.

In chapter 6 we noted how friendship requires time and space apart where conversation is encouraged, argument is tolerated, and people have enough time truly to know one another. Thus matters relating to space for constant conversation and interaction are not small matters. The concern, on the part of many students and faculty, for places to eat together and to converse together is a concern about the foundation of our life as an educational community.

8. Brown, p. 60.

148

Because, in the words of Montaigne, "Friendship feeds on communications," if we want friendship to be the basis of our life together we must foster those settings and opportunities where there can be much conversation and intellectual conviviality of the sort advocated by Reynolds Price. Jane Tomkins has led a movement to establish two new coffee bars on the Duke campus. To date, these coffee bars have quickly become centers of conversation and the productive "hanging out" that Tompkins said Duke needed.

Montaigne doubts that there can be true friendship between parents and children, because of their inequality. Perhaps he would say the same of faculty and students. Inequality is inimical to friendship because inequality inhibits correction and discipline, one of the chief duties of friendship, for Montaigne. Yet even within the necessary constraints of the student-teacher relationship — or perhaps one should say *especially* because of the demands of the student-teacher relationship — friendship is an adequate metaphor for what we want to happen between faculty and students. Many of us have good friends who are unequal to us in terms of age, income, or experience. These inequalities can be overcome, can even be a positive source of friendly interaction within friendship.

In our first chapter we leveled much criticism at Greek life on campus. There is indeed much to criticize, especially among our fraternities. Yet for all their faults, fraternities play an important role in many students' lives. Sororities and fraternities are criticized, but many first-year students find that they *need* to enter a fraternity or a sorority to have a sense of themselves, a sense that anybody out there cares about them. The meaningless Greek letters of the fraternity give them a sense of belonging.

Our main criticism of Greek life is on those campuses where passive administrators and students have allowed it to monopolize student social life. The Greek system provides one of the few places, though fortunately not the only place, where students can be together in face-to-face, intimate, sustained ways. In short, fraternities are an experiment in friendship. At Duke, we are pleased that there has been a concerted effort to encourage a plethora of groupings — a dorm for environmentalists, a dorm where cultural diversity is explored and enhanced, a dorm for artists and musicians, a dorm for those who want to experiment in organizing themselves to foster community — whereby our students might experience more ownership and control of their lives on campus and might be forced to be with a diversity of students within sustained, deep encounters, where they might learn to be friends with people who once were strangers.

Interestingly, when Will spent a semester talking about academic reform issues on the Duke campus with students in their living groups and dormitories, he noted that the conversation within the fraternities and sororities tended to be more incisive, more honest, and more focused than conversations in our "random," lottery housing dormitories. It really made a difference to have people in conversation who actually knew one another.

Campus life can be reformed only if we encourage and cultivate a wide array of productive campus groups. Religious life groups, as well as social and political action groups, make a great contribution to the development and maturity of our students. Duke, for instance, has thirteen different campus religious groups, each with an adult campus minister advising them. Every week, fifty Bible study groups meet on the Duke campus, providing members with intimate, face-to-face interaction.

At the same time, administrators should unashamedly discourage nonproductive groups and encourage the productive ones. After an extensive survey of disciplinary problems on today's campus, David A. Hoekema concludes that the answer lies not in more detailed or strict codes of conduct but rather in fostering better groups on campus:

> One of the persistent themes of recent work in moral philosophy is the indispensable role of community in shaping our moral universe. . . . We learn to be moral by modeling ourselves on others whose judgment and integrity we respect . . . to rely on ever more strenuous enforcement of disciplinary rules and codes is an inherently ill-suited tactic, if one's goal is to assist students to become mature and responsible moral agents. Institutions ought rather to devote their efforts to systematic encouragement

of the smaller communities contained on campus in which moral reflection and thoughtful choice flourish.[9]

There is considerable disagreement among social scientists and others as to whether or not *exclusivity* is a prerequisite for community. Should membership in a learning community be open to all comers or be tightly controlled? We believe that, yes, colleges and universities aspiring to be communities must be exclusive — exclusively committed to those who desire an education as defined by the university. We cannot be all things to all people. The student whose lifetime goal is a pro football career should be encouraged to pursue that career, but not at a college where education is that student's minor concern. A community must be able to identify itself, to discern who is in and who is not in that community. Colleges and universities tolerate illegal and immoral behavior on their campuses because they appear to have lost the means to say to some students, "By your behavior you have shown that you no longer belong in a community whose major purpose is education." Likewise, we tolerate faculty whose entrepreneurial style and absence from the campus ought to lead us to say, "You have demonstrated that you no longer belong in a community whose major purpose is teaching."

Real communities must also be grounded on a foundation of *equality* and *justice*. However, in no sense are we suggesting that all members of a community must think and act exactly alike. One major shortcoming of the current "diversity" movement on college campuses is that it sometimes breeds conformity rather than diversity. It may actually impede the development of academic community as students huddle in their own cultural enclave, smugly secure in their "culture." Furthermore, if a residential college is dominated by the faculty or administration, with little power given to the students, it will never evolve into a true learning community.

9. David A. Hoekema, *Campus Rules and Moral Community: In Place of In Loco Parentis* (Lanham, Md.: Rowman & Littlefield Pub., 1994), p. 159.

The Last Best Hope

It is greatly to the advantage of Gingrich and Robertson to convince the public that the colleges and universities — the places where blacks and gays, women and recent immigrants are treated best — are eccentric, dissolute, corrupt, and perverse. This enables them to dismiss out of hand the warnings of liberal professors — warnings about creating an underclass without hope and of letting the national agenda be dominated by the fears of the suburbs. Such warnings can be brushed aside by treating the academy as having succumbed to a "modish, leftist, moralistic liberalism." We can expect, in the next few years, to see more and more attempts to discredit the colleges and universities, for the right is well aware that the American academy is now (after the breakdown of the labor movement) the last remaining defender of the poor against the rich and of the weak against the strong.[10]

Empowerment is another important community attribute. American colleges and universities have traditionally been organized in a hierarchical fashion with the faculty and administration sharing little power with students. Yet in a real community the power to shape and influence the direction of the group must be shared by all members.

The real question is, How much and what kind of power ought we to share with students? Power sharing can be very threatening to academic administrators. On the other hand, it is difficult to engender student-faculty trust without giving students a piece of the action. We have no basic formula for academic power sharing. But

10. Richard Rorty, "A Leg-up for Oliver North," *London Review of Books,* October 20, 1994.

if corporate managers can learn to share power with their employees, as is quite often the case in Europe and Japan, why can't American college administrators draw more students into the academic decision-making process?

One thing is for sure — community cannot be mandated from above by the administration or the faculty. Real community is a bottom-up process requiring the full participation of both faculty and students.

Two other noteworthy features of communities are *adaptability* and *conflict resolution*. In order to survive, a learning community must be able to adapt to a changing external environment and to resolve its own internal conflicts. Each learning community needs some sort of conflict resolution mechanism to reduce tensions when disputes arise among students or between faculty and students. Obviously, the more open the communication between faculty and students, the smaller the number of persons to be included in the debate, the easier it is to resolve conflicts resulting from academic diversity and pluralism.

Alas, the search for academic communities yields few positive examples and an overwhelming number of institutions where community has completely broken down, if it ever existed there. We feel privileged to be at campuses, Middlebury and Duke, where administrators and students are engaged in a substantive discussion about how best to foster community on campus. While we await more faculty involvement on this issue, we are pleased that Middlebury and Duke are assuming leadership. On too many of our campuses, the administration is still in a state of denial, failing to see their responsibility to foster student community.

Both television and the automobile have contributed to the breakdown of community on college campuses. One keeps students glued to the privacy of their dormitory room; the other draws many of them to the road. Neither does much to build community. When students want to go to a movie, a pub, a restaurant, the post office, or a shopping mall, they hop in the car and drive. Often there are few places where faculty and students meet — whether on campus or in a nearby neighborhood — just to talk, have a coffee, and contemplate the meaning of life. High-rise dormitories and their moribund parking lots are evidence of our inhumanity and loss of community.

Why does community elude us in the academy? How is it possible for something that we claim to cherish so dearly to be found so seldom in the real world? Everybody talks about community, but few faculty members are willing to pay the price in terms of foregone narcissism and individualism necessary for community.

The essence of our free-enterprise capitalistic system involves promoting the virtues of individualism — often subordinating the interests of the community to those of the individual. The Japanese, on the other hand, take a quite different view of the relationship between the individual and the community. In Japanese companies, for example, the interests of the CEO are subordinated to those of the employees and the customers. The well-being of the group or the community always takes precedence over individual self-interest. Profits are considered to be a reward bestowed on the company by society for doing a good job rather than an entitlement. So accustomed are most Americans to looking out for number one that they find the loss of control implied by genuine community to be very threatening.

Not unrelated to our obsession with individualism is our fondness for authoritarian management. Many large American corporations are among the least democratic institutions in the world. So too is the case with the administration at our colleges and universities, nonprofit institutions, and government at all levels. Most European companies and universities are much more participatory in their management practices than their American counterparts.

Kirkpatrick Sale, in his book *Human Scale,* has compiled considerable evidence to suggest that sheer size alone is an important determination of the long-term viability of human community. Sale believes there is a size limit beyond which a community should not be allowed to grow if it is to survive. He even goes so far as to propose optimum size limits for what he calls a *neighborhood* and a *standard community.* Sale defines a neighborhood as a group of between four hundred and one thousand people — a face-to-face community such as an Alpine village, a section of a large city, or a residential college. His suggestion that five hundred people may represent an optimum size for a neighborhood is compatible with our notion of a residential college (see chapter 7). A standard community, on the other hand, is an extended group of people consisting of a collection of neighborhoods. A college or a small university with five thousand students would be consistent with Sale's definition of a standard community.

Although there is only limited experience with the residential college system in the United States, we believe this academic model affords us a good opportunity for creating sustainable learning communities. Obviously, creating learning communities in new residential colleges with no previous history or experience with community will be a challenging task. However, if three hundred or so students live together in a common residential area — not in a high-rise dormitory — where they eat together, play together, and learn together, with significant faculty participation, some semblance of community will eventually emerge.

Clearly, college administrators cannot mandate community and expect students and faculty to fall into place. But they can create structures far more conducive to community than the present ill-conceived, ill-planned hodgepodge of dehumanized dormitories, military-style food service, and mass-production classroom buildings all under the umbrella of a live-and-let-live philosophy where students and faculty each go their own way. At least on the surface, the residential college system is far more user-friendly to undergraduates than the anachronistic university system that dominates higher education in America today.

As one example of what is possible when students, faculty, administrators, and alumni work together in a residential college environment, consider Princeton's response to its alcohol-abuse problem. Shortly after the intoxicated Princeton sophomore was electrocuted in 1990, Princeton president Harold Shapiro asked O. Carl Wartenburg, an administrative assistant and popular campus figure, to work on alcohol abuse full time. Shapiro charged Wartenburg with "assisting students to see the problem of abuse as their problem, and enlisting their involvement in education and prevention programs."[11]

With a grant from the Department of Education, Wartenburg began a comprehensive approach to alcohol abuse. Instead of drawing up new rules for students, he placed the students' needs and experiences at the center of his alcohol initiative. After a number of years of shunning all negative publicity related to alcohol abuse, the university reversed its policy and began directing attention loudly and publicly to the campus problem with alcohol. The administration's strategy was to show students that it cared more about their welfare than keeping embarrassing news out of the papers. Wartenburg, dubbed the "alcohol czar," roamed the campus for eighteen months, gathering information, talking to students, visiting their places of social interaction. Then he devised a threefold strategy. First, he consulted with students and others about the causes and results of excessive drinking; second, using the data collected, there was a public attempt to explode the illusions about campus life and to expose the seamier side to public gaze; and third, a corporate strategy was devised to alleviate the problems. Wartenburg, in discussions with students, found that many students wished that alcohol were less central to social activities. Many factors prompted students to drink excessively, factors having to do with the complexity of campus culture. He concluded that the best way to change drinking patterns was through peer pressure. Therefore he collaborated with students and administrators to devise social alternatives to keg parties.

Wartenburg confessed to an administrative abdication of responsibilities outside the classroom: "This initiative is about the quality of undergraduate life, and that includes all of the ways in which people relate and grow." Wartenburg asserted that "the educational outcomes we seek to foster are moral, spiritual, emotional, and physical, as well as intellectual. Right now, we do a great job from the shoulders up."

11. D. W. Miller, "Saying When: Princeton Faces Its Drinking Problem," *Princeton Alumni Weekly*, November 25, 1992, pp. 7-9.

From the very beginning, at freshman orientation (which was characterized at Princeton as a "five-day drunk"), freshmen were introduced into an alcohol-centered culture. At first-year orientation, Wartenburg fashioned a slate of nonalcoholic events every night of the week, including late-night athletic activities in the gym. He even opened a pub in the student center, convinced that drinking under controlled circumstances is better than overdrinking freely in clubs and dorms. (An earlier pub had closed in 1985, two years after the rise of the drinking age put a huge dent in its business.)

Confronting the Princeton drinking clubs for their behavior, discussing the issue openly, Wartenburg got most clubs to agree not to hold parties during orientation week; and they also agreed to bar freshmen at the door.

Interestingly, President Shapiro also confronted the issue of alumni reunions. In the students' minds, excessive drinking by alumni made administrative efforts to curb student alcohol abuse look hypocritical. Shapiro announced a one-year ban on beer kegs on the campus. Major reunion officers had to negotiate with the ban, submitting plans for restricting access and availability of beer at their reunion parties. Mainly, the one-year ban served to draw people's attention to the problem and show administrative seriousness related to the issue.

Shapiro sponsored a two-day convention of sorts among Princeton alumni, students, local businesses, and others concerned about the problem — the Alcohol Congress on Responsible Decisions (ACORD). The alcohol-abuse initiatives at Duke, Washington and Lee, Michigan, and elsewhere are impressive, showing that a new generation of college administrators is no longer in denial regarding this pressing student health issue.

One of the more obvious advantages of the residential college system is that it can provide students with a stronger sense of place than is usually the case in large, impersonal "dormitories." Students eat, sleep, play, and learn within the confines of a relatively small, well-defined space. This space is their space for the four years they are at college.

However, the college as a whole should also encourage activities conducive to interaction among residential colleges, such as intramural sports, drama, musical groups, literary clubs, religious organizations, a campus newspaper, varsity sports, and community volunteerism.

A relatively new face in students' academic lives is community volunteer service. At Duke, Middlebury, UVM, and many other places a very high percentage of students contribute one to ten hours of volunteer service to their local community every week. For many of these students, their volunteer experiences provide important insights and personal growth. Unfortunately, relatively few professors are available to encourage students in their community work or help them process their experiences. Perhaps this is because students may be much more generous with their time and talents in the local community than are faculty.

Student Volunteerism

It is estimated that 25 percent of all college students now volunteer an average of five hours a week for community-service projects. Recent polls indicate the percentage of Americans between the ages of 18 and 24 who volunteer at least a day of their time during the course of a year has risen significantly since 1988.[12]

---

12. "What If Nobody Cared? Volunteerism Is Becoming a Staple of Student Life," *Syracuse University Magazine*, Fall 1994, pp. 14-17. See the extensive discussion of student volunteerism and its motivating factors in Paul Rogat Loeb, *A Generation at the Crossroads: Apathy and Action on the American Campus* (New Brunswick, N.J.: Rutgers University Press, 1994), pp. 127-248. See also Derek Bok, *Beyond the Ivory Tower: Social Responsibilities of the Modern University* (Cambridge: Harvard University Press, 1982).

As an alternative to stricter college control of alcohol consumption, we propose tougher student course loads, an expanded range of college-sponsored activities, as well as evening, Saturday, and early-morning classes and increased faculty-student interaction.

For new colleges resulting from the downsizing of universities, the creation of residential colleges may prove to be much easier than is the case with already existing colleges. For example, at Middlebury College, most students are opposed to converting Middlebury Commons into full-fledged residential colleges. As a result of inadequate consultation with students on the evolution of commons, many Middlebury students actually favor a return to the fraternity-sorority system recently abandoned by the college.

The negative response of Middlebury students to the proposed residential college model raises the question of the role of students and faculty in the governance of a college. It will come as no great surprise that we strongly favor making college governance much more participatory. Although the board of trustees is ultimately responsible for the consequences of all college policies, the policy-making process should involve faculty, students, and administrators. Just as Japanese and European companies have embraced management-employee teams, so too should colleges rely more on faculty-student-administration teams.

Duke's successful Center for Teaching and Learning found that students learn best in participatory environments where they have a hand in the direction of their education. So many of the innovative programs that have been initiated at Duke (including the Center for Teaching and Learning itself) have been the results of student action. Notable programs that make our university better — to recycle refuse on campus, to collect surplus food and distribute it to the local soup kitchen, to install campus bikeways, to call for the establishment of a new School of the Environment — were student-initiated. These Duke students will be well prepared to take a leadership role in the corporations, universities, hospitals, and businesses where they will work in the future.

Above all, the faculty must assume more responsibility and play a more proactive role in the creation and maintenance of college learning communities. They should exert more energy in confronting and engaging students rather than cowering to their every whim. Faculty must become involved in the discussion of student life on campus. The unintended result of higher standards and increased professionalization for student-affairs personnel "has been the erosion of any sense of shared responsibility for matters of student conduct."[13]

There are no shortcuts to community and participatory management. When Duke's president, Nan Keohane, determined to receive much student input regarding the new housing proposals at Duke, the process was laborious, time-consuming, and at times, exhausting. But the end result was unquestionably better than if a cadre of top administrators had decided the housing plan. It is much more difficult to manage through teams rather than by executive decree. However, the world is changing. American business is already in a more participatory, team-directed, total quality management mode. Is there any other alternative? We must find ways to empower our students, to impress upon them their responsibility for the state of their futures. Maya Angelou told a convocation of Duke's first-year students this past fall, "You have been the beneficiaries of a great educational system. This society has given you the best it has in the way of advantages, opportunities, and growth. Now, as the privileged elite, you owe us something!"

The success of college learning communities will depend heavily on the strength of the college's leadership and the commitment of the faculty. A committed faculty can turn around apathetic students, but not vice versa.

A rich undergraduate intellectual experience cannot come from two or three hours in the classroom once a week. It requires a climate in which faculty and students alike see

13. Hoekema, p. 145.

Duke as a place for shared discovery, for conversation, for intellectual and personal connections that stimulate new thought and action.[14]

In summary and conclusion, we call this nation's campuses to an adventurous process of reform and reinvention of American higher education. Every time we walk into our classrooms at Duke or Middlebury, we realize anew how great a trust has been committed to our care. We are privileged to live and to work among some of this nation's most talented youth. If we are unable to address our problems, to create a learning community where people care for one another's intellectual development, what hope can there be for this society as a whole, so dependent as it is upon the future leadership that is produced by our colleges and universities? To stem the tide of the crisis in undergraduate higher education, we therefore propose eight strategies to create college communities of scholars and teachers:

1. *Downsizing:* Downsize universities by spinning off undergraduate education to smaller satellite colleges.
2. *Residential Colleges:* Introduce a system of residential colleges into existing colleges and newly created ones.
3. *Teaching:* Require undergraduate professors to teach at least three or four courses per semester.
4. *Tenure:* Replace the tenure system with a system of long-term contracts.
5. *Curricula:* Reduce the freedom available to undergraduates in their choice of courses.
6. *Course Load:* Increase the number of academic courses required each semester to graduate from four to five.

14. Duke President Nannerl O. Keohane, in *The Duke Dialogue,* October 28, 1994, p. 7.

7. *Learning Communities:* Create sustainable learning communities within residential colleges.
8. *Participation:* Make college policymaking more participatory so that students, faculty, and administrators are included in the process.

After decades of distancing ourselves from our students, abandoning them to their own devices, we are hopeful that American colleges and universities can recover a sense of themselves as intellectual and moral communities dedicated to the mutual pursuit of knowledge and character. Our students deserve nothing less.

The Search for Meaning

(as taught at Middlebury College)

"The Search is what anyone would undertake if he were not sunk in the everydayness in his life. To become aware of the possibility of the search is to be onto something. Not to be onto something is to be in despair," said Walker Percy in *The Moviegoer*. This course provides a conceptual framework and process to facilitate the search for meaning that attempts to integrate the spiritual, intellectual, emotional, and physiological dimensions of life. Meaninglessness, separation, having, and being are among the scenarios for meaning considered. Tools for the search include philosophy, religion, psychotherapy, literature, women's studies, and fine arts. Each class session is 2½ hours.

Schedule

Session 1   *Introduction*
The Living Dead
The Fable of the Deserted Island
Norman Lear (Video)

Reading
Text & Workbook, Introduction

Session 2   *A Search Process*
               The Life Matrix
               Meaninglessness
               Ecclesiastes
               Chopin's Funeral March (audiotape)

               Reading
               Text & Workbook, chapters 1-2
               Camus, *The Stranger*

Session 3   *Separation*
               The Story of Johnny and Sasha
               Freedom and Destiny
               Isolation

               Reading
               Text & Workbook, chapter 3
               May, *Freedom and Destiny*
               Peck, *The Road Less Traveled,* chapter 1

Session 4   *Death*

               Reading
               Becker, *The Denial of Death*

Session 5   *Having*
               Ground Hog Day (video)

               Reading
               Text & Workbook, chapter 4
               Fromm, *To Have or to Be*

Session 6   *Being*
               1. Our Creations
               2. Love Relationships
               3. Pain and Suffering

Reading
Text & Workbook, chapter 5
Frankl, *Man's Search for Meaning*
Fromm, *To Have or to Be*
Gorbachev, *I Hope*
Hillesum, *An Interrupted Life*
Kundera, *The Unbearable Lightness of Being*
Peck, *The Road Less Traveled,* chapter 2
Tillich, *The Courage to Be*

Session 7   *Women and the Search*

Reading
Dozier and Adams, *Sisters and Brothers*
Farley, *Tragic Vision and Divine Compassion*
Hillesum, *An Interrupted Life*
Kolbenschlag, *Kiss Sleeping Beauty Good-Bye*
Koller, *An Unknown Woman*
Lorde, *Sister Outsider*
Welch, *Communities of Resistance and Solidarity*

Session 8   *Personal Philosophy*
1. Meaning
2. Values
3. Ethics
4. Social Responsibility

Reading
Text & Workbook, chapter 6
May, *Freedom and Destiny*
Peck, *The Road Less Traveled*

Session 9   *The Longing for Community*

Reading
Text & Workbook, chapter 7

Red and White Colours of Switzerland (video)
Vermont (video)

Session 10   *Psychotherapy, Biopsychiatry, and Medicine*

Reading
Text, pages 185-90
Workbook, chapter 9
Cousins, *Anatomy of an Illness as Perceived by the Patient*
Yalom, *When Nietzsche Wept*

Session 12   *Literature*
1. Leo Tolstoy, *The Death of Ivan Ilych*
2. Joseph Conrad, *Heart of Darkness*
3. Henry James, *The Best of the Jungle*
4. Franz Kafka, *The Metamorphosis*
5. Miguel de Uanmuno y Jugo, *Abel Sanchez*
6. Andre Gide, *The Pastoral Symphony*
7. Thomas Mann, *Mario and the Magician*
8. William Faulkner, *Old Man*
9. Albert Camus, *The Stranger*
10. Richard Wright, *The Man Who Lived Underground*
11. Alberto Moravia, *Agostino*
12. Mary Gordon, *Final Payments*
13. Barbara Kingsolver, *Animal Dreams*
14. Alice Walker, *Meridian*
15. Sylvia Plath, *The Bell Jar*

Reading
Text, pages 193-96

Session 13   *Religion*

Reading

Text, pages 201-5
Noddings, *Educating for Intelligent Belief or Unbelief*

Session 14   *Soul Crafting*
             Happy Death

             Reading
             Text & Workbook, chapter 10

Session 15   *Fine Arts* (Class Project)
             Music
             Painting
             Sculpture
             Dance
             Film
             Drama

             Reading
             Text, pages 196-200

Text & Workbook:

1. Naylor, Thomas H., William H. Willimon, and Magdalena R. Naylor. *The Search for Meaning*. Nashville: Abingdon, 1994.
2. ———. *The Search for Meaning Workbook*. Nashville: Abingdon, 1994.

Required Reading:

1. Frankl, Viktor E. *Man's Search for Meaning*. New York: Washington Square, 1984.
2. Hillesum, Etty. *An Interrupted Life*. New York: Washington Square, 1985.

3. Yalom, Irvin D. *When Nietzsche Wept.* New York: Basic Books, 1992.

Evaluation Criteria:

Class Participation
Personal History (5 pages)
Biographical Sketch (5 pages)
Personal Philosophy (5 pages)
Personal Strategy (5 pages)

Bibliography:

1. Becker, Ernest. *The Denial of Death.* New York: Free Press, 1973.
2. Berman, Phillip L. *The Search for Meaning.* New York: Ballantine Books, 1990.
3. Camus, Albert. *The Stranger.* New York: Knopf, 1946.
4. ———. *The Plague.* New York: Knopf, 1948.
5. ———. *The Myth of Sisyphus.* New York: Knopf, 1955.
6. ———. *A Happy Death.* New York: Knopf, 1972.
7. Cousins, Norman. *Anatomy of an Illness as Perceived by the Patient.* New York: Norton, 1979.
8. Dozier, Verna J., and James R. Adams. *Sisters and Brothers.* Cambridge: Cowley, 1993.
9. Farley, Wendy. *Tragic Vision and Divine Compassion: A Contemporary Theodicy.* Louisville: Westminster, 1990.
10. Frankl, Viktor E. *Man's Search for Meaning.* New York: Washington Square, 1984.
11. Friend, David, ed. *The Meaning of Life.* Boston: Little, Brown, 1991.
12. Fromm, Erich. *To Have or to Be.* New York: Bantam Books, 1981.
13. Gorbachev, Raisa. *I Hope.* New York: Harper Collins, 1991.

14. Hamilton, Leo, and Edmond Volpe, eds. *Eleven Modern Short Novels*. New York: Putnam, 1970.
15. Kolbenschlag, M. *Kiss Sleeping Beauty Good-Bye*. New York: Doubleday, 1979.
16. Koller, Alice. *An Unknown Woman*. New York: Bantam Books, 1987.
17. Kundera, Milan. *The Unbearable Lightness of Being*. New York: Harper & Row, 1984.
18. Lorde, Audre. *Sister Outsider*. Trumansburg, N.Y.: Crossing Press, 1984.
19. May, Rollo. *Freedom and Destiny*. New York: Dell, 1981.
20. Miller, Arthur. *Death of a Salesman*. New York: Penguin Books, 1976.
21. Noddings, Nel. *Educating for Intelligent Belief or Unbelief*. New York: Teachers College Press, 1993.
22. O'Neill, Eugene. *The Iceman Cometh*. New York: Vantage, 1957.
23. Peck, M. Scott. *The Road Less Traveled*. New York: Touchstone, 1978.
24. Percy, Walker. *The Moviegoer*. New York: Ballantine Books, 1960.
25. Tillich, Paul. *The Courage to Be*. New Haven, Ct.: Yale, 1952.
26. Welch, Sharon. *Communities of Resistance and Solidarity: A Feminist Theology of Liberation*. Maryknoll, N.Y.: Orbis, 1985.
27. Yalom, Irvin D. *Existential Psychotherapy*. New York: Basic Books, 1980.

Index of Names

Index of Names

Keohane, Nannerl O., 83, 126, 160-61
Kerr, Clark, 93, 146
Kimball, Roger, 91
King, Martin Luther, Jr., 55
Kohlberg, Lawrence, 28
Kohr, Leopold, 72, 80
Krzyzewski, Mike, 77

Layd, William, 86
Leo, John, 22
Levine, Arthur, 86, 87
Levinson, Daniel, 89
Loeb, Paul Rogat, 26, 27, 57, 66, 91, 92, 116, 140, 158
Lonergan, Bernard J., 46
Long, Edward LeRoy, Jr., 43, 63, 65, 88, 143, 146

Marcus, Jon, 101
McCrate, E. S., 117
Miller, D. W., 5, 156
Montaigne, 149

Naylor, Magdelena R., 145
Naylor, Susanne, 102
Naylor, Thomas H., 44, 63, 67, 114, 145
Newman, John Henry Cardinal, 144

Oakley, Francis, 115, 128

Parks, Sharon, 88
Perley, James, 101

Pepper, Meredith, 134
Percy, Walker, 50, 51
Peters, R. S., 27
Plato, 57, 67, 68, 80
Postman, Neil, 56, 57, 90, 135
Price, Reynolds, 4, 23, 60, 111, 149

Reno, Robert, 101
Rorty, Richard, 152
Rudolph, Frederick, 128, 141

Sale, Kirkpatrick, 154-55
Sams, Ferrol, 3
Sharp, Ronald A., 93
Silber, John, 102
Sloan, Douglas, 135
Shapiro, Harold, 6, 155, 157
Smith, Adam, 51
Smith, B. H., 115, 128
Smith, Dean, 9, 75
Strauss, William, 51

Tocqueville, Alexis de, 90
Tompkins, Jane, 144-45, 149

Veblen, Thorstein, 31

Wartenburg, O. Carl, 155-57
Waugh, Evelyn, 19
Wechsler, Henry, 7, 10
Welty, Eudora, 93
Wessells, Norman, 22
Willimon, William H., xii, 63, 67, 145, 150